# One

Mark Weis

Mark Weis
*One Thing Needful – Volume 2*

Copyright 2018 by Mark Weis

# ACKNOWLEDGEMENTS

Many thanks to Craig F. Owings
for editing this book,
to Matt Schaser for designing the covers,
and to Michael Roehl for reviewing the content.

You are all good friends
and gifts to God's Church.
Even with my love of writing,
I don't have enough words to thank you.

# PREFACE

I published the first volume of *One Thing Needful* in May of 2017. Since that time, many of you have sent notes of encouragement, thanking me for writing the book, and sharing ways and places you've used it—hospital rooms, family devotions, Christian schools; and in one instance, a missionary trip to Africa.

If the book has helped you, I'm truly grateful. I'm even more grateful that God has used my words to glorify His.

And I pray that the second volume of *One Thing Needful* will serve the same purposes: God's glory and your encouragement. Like the first volume, the second is devotional in nature, though its devotions are somewhat longer and meatier. I hope you won't mind.

You'll also notice that the devotions are divided into four sections. The first and longest section is composed of general devotions; the second, devotions on the seven letters to the seven churches in Revelation; the third, the seven times Jesus spoke from the cross; and the fourth, the seven petitions of the Lord's Prayer.

As you likely know, the title *One Thing Needful* is based on the words of Jesus to Martha in Luke 10:41-42, "Martha, Martha, you are worried and troubled about many things. But *one thing is needed*, and Mary has chosen that good part, which will not be taken away from her."

We remember the setting: The home of Mary, Martha, and Lazarus in Bethany. Mary sitting, listening to Jesus teach. Martha busily preparing dinner. I don't know why, but I always envision Martha wearing a checkered apron with MARTHA'S KITCHEN embroidered on the front. I see her stirring and sampling pots, adding seasoning, adjusting the heat. I see her aligning place settings and wiping a smudge off the silverware.

Most of all, I see Martha racing between the kitchen and dining room, red-cheeked and flustered, wiping a sweaty bang from her forehead, and casting angry glances at her sister Mary—until she blurts in exasperation, "Lord, do You not care that my sister has left me to serve alone? Therefore tell her to help me."

Honestly, I've always felt sorry for Martha. Like her siblings, Martha loved Jesus and wanted to please Him. It was important to her that dinner preparations be perfect. And who can blame her? After all, her Dinner Guest that day was none other than the Son of God.

Martha wasn't a bad person. Martha was a distracted person—distracted from the Word of God. Her wholesome desire to feed Jesus interfered with His desire to feed her. And so in great love, Jesus reminded Martha, "You are worried and troubled about many things. But only one thing is needed."

The lesson is clear, isn't it? There are many important things in life. Yet, one thing trumps them all: the hearing of God's Word. While I could offer many Bible passages to support this statement, I think one will suffice: "So then faith comes by hearing, and hearing by the word of God," Romans 10:17.

May the Lord Jesus bless you, your loved ones, and your reading.

*Mark Weis*
September 4, 2018

# CONTENTS

# Abraham's Journey of Faith

Genesis 12:1-8

*Abraham is important in Scripture, not because of who he was, but because of the One in Whom he believed.*

The Book of Genesis spans 2,246 years, or approximately one-third of all human history. Two thousand of those years are contained in the first eleven chapters—primarily in the genealogies of Genesis 5, 10, and 11.

By contrast, the remaining thirty-eight chapters of Genesis cover a period of 246 years. With the first words of Genesis 12, the divine record slows with the calling of Abraham. Why? The answer is simple. Abraham is of great importance to much of what follows in Scripture, culminating with the coming of Jesus Christ. He is also a foundational example of justification by faith alone, and what it means to trust God to keep His word.

Abraham's life was a journey of faith. The essence of faith does not change, as defined in Hebrews 11:1, "Now faith is the substance of things hoped for, the evidence of things not seen." Likewise, Almighty God does not change, as He Himself stated in Malachi 3:6, "For I am the LORD, I do not change." And these two facts, the unchanging nature of faith and the unchanging faithfulness of God, are what make our journey through life no less incredible than Abraham's.

**The Call of God**

Imagine being seventy-five years old, happily married, and solidly into retirement. You're living in a city called Haran, a city of palm trees and ample water and fertile soil. Regrettably, you and your wife Sarah have no children; but you do have servants, livestock, and great wealth. Life is good. You're happy and content. You and your wife Sarah, now sixty-five herself, enjoy Haran and enjoy the life you've built together.

Given such circumstances, how likely are you to one day announce, "Honey, I've made a decision." Your wife says, "I'm listening." You say, "I've decided that we should leave Haran and journey to Canaan." She says, "Where's Canaan?" You say, "About five hundred miles from here." She says, "Wait. Let me get this straight. You want us to gather all our belongings, and for Lot and family to do the same—tents, clothes, food, water, pots and pans, dishes and silverware, knickknacks, livestock; to leave our home, and at our age to set out on a five-hundred-mile journey that, even if we managed ten miles a day, would take fifty days? Have you lost your mind?"

Did this conversation take place? Doubtful, at least in a patriarchal society. But who knows? In any case, the dialogue illustrates how unlikely Abraham would have been to make such a journey on his own. His journey of faith was not possible, not started, not even contemplated, until he received a call to faith from God. "Now the LORD had said to Abram: 'Get out of your country, from your family and from your father's house, to a land that I will show you," Genesis 12:1.

Our call to faith came from God, too. Our journey to faith in Christ was not our choice, but the result of God's call. This is why Paul repeatedly referred to his Christian readers as those "called" by God. For example, he wrote in 1 Corinthians 1:9, "God is faithful, by whom you were *called* into the fellowship of His Son, Jesus Christ our Lord."

And our call to faith is no less miraculous, no less incredible, than Abraham's. You may think, "Well, God didn't appear to me in the same way he appeared to Abraham." That is true. But the essence of God's call to Abraham was through His word. "The LORD had *said* to Abram," Genesis 12:1. God appeared to you, came to you, in exactly the same way; namely, through His Word, the Bible.

Oh, that we would remember this when we're young and disillusioned or old and regretful: "God chose me. God called me to make this journey of faith. God promised to bless me through this journey and be with me as I travel. And what my God has called me to do, He will empower me to do."

## The Grace and Power of God

"Get out of your country, from your family and from your father's house, to a land that *I* will show you. *I* will make you a great nation; *I* will bless you and make your name great; and you shall be a blessing. *I* will bless those who bless you, and *I* will curse him who curses you; and in you all the families of the earth shall be blessed," Genesis 12:1-3.

How many times did God say "I" in these verses? Five times. From the outset of the journey, what was God telling Abraham? "I called you to go. I will get you there." Can you think of anything more comforting to a 75-year-old man, who was about to leave the familiar for the unknown?

This is easily overlooked. But did you realize that Abraham actually set out for Canaan twice? The first journey was at the direction of his father, Terah. According to Genesis 11:31, "And Terah took his son Abram and his grandson Lot, the son of Haran, and his daughter-in-law Sarai, his son Abram's wife, and they went out with them from Ur of the Chaldeans to go to the land of Canaan; and they came to Haran and dwelt there."

Instructive, isn't it? When Abraham left for Canaan on his own, he didn't make it. He quite literally *settled* for someplace else. But when he believed God's word and obeyed God's call, God got Abraham safely to the Promised Land.

We wonder at times, "How am I going to make it? How am I going to make it through all these bills, through this illness, through this difficult ministry or troubled marriage, through this loss of a loved one? O Lord God, how am I going to make it to eternal life—through one more day, one more problem, one more worry?"

Scripturally, there is but one answer to each of these questions. And the answer is, "Almighty God." The answer is the same answer given to Abraham: "I will bless you and make your name great; and you shall be a blessing," Genesis 12:2. The answer is in 1 Thessalonians 5:24, "He who calls you is faithful, who also will do it."

## God's Reliable Word

At its simplest, faith is taking God at His word. This Abraham did again and again—when traveling from Ur of the Chaldeans to Canaan, when waiting twenty years for the birth of Isaac, when preparing to sacrifice Isaac at God's command.

Think of all the impossibilities Abraham faced. Though God had promised Canaan to this patriarch and his descendants, Abraham did not legally own one square inch of the Promised Land to the day he died—except for the Cave of Machpelah, where both Abraham and Sarah were buried.

So we ask, how could Abraham patiently overcome all the obstacles and impossibilities of his incredible journey? And we hear the Spirit of God answer, "And he believed in the LORD, and He accounted it to him for righteousness," Genesis 15:6. Or as Paul explained in Romans 4:20-21, speaking of Abraham: "He did not waver at the promise of God through unbelief, but was strengthened in faith, giving glory to God, and being fully convinced that what He had promised He was also able to perform."

The nature of faith is unchanging. The faithfulness of God is unchanging. This is what makes our journey through life no different from that of Abraham's.

# A Miraculous Meal

Matthew 14:13-21

*Of all the miracles Jesus performed during His earthly ministry, only the Feeding of the Five Thousand is recorded in all four Gospels. Why?*

Jesus performed many miracles. He healed the sick. He controlled the weather and walked on water. He cast out demons and changed water into wine. He raised the dead: Lazarus, the daughter of Jairus, and the son of the widow from Nain. Jesus performed these miracles not only to help and heal, to restore and liberate; but also to prove that He was exactly Who He claimed to be: the Son of God and the only Savior of lost humanity.

Yet, the miracles of Jesus recorded in the New Testament are only a small percentage of all His miraculous deeds. The apostle John wrote, "And truly Jesus did many other signs in the presence of His disciples, which are not written in this book; but these are written that you may believe that Jesus is the Christ, the Son of God, and that believing you may have life in His name," John 20:30-31.

Of all Christ's miracles, however, only one is recorded in all four Gospels: Matthew 14, Mark 6, Luke 9, and John 6. And that one miracle is the *Feeding of the Five Thousand.* Why this fourfold repetition? Why is this miracle recorded four times, when the *Feeding of the Four Thousand* is recorded only twice—and when an astonishing miracle like the resurrection of Lazarus is recorded only once?

Interesting questions, with no direct answer provided in Scripture. Yet, perhaps the answer is as simple as this: in the *Feeding of the Five Thousand*, we learn so many comforting truths about our Savior, and we learn them not in an extraordinary context like a cemetery at Bethany or a tempestuous storm on Lake Galilee, but in a context as commonplace as our daily need to eat.

## The Savior's Compassion

At times, even we are tempted to doubt God's compassion. "God, why did You let this happen to me—this illness, this accident, this loss, this broken marriage, foreclosure, bankruptcy, automobile accident?" Yet, God does have the utmost compassion for us, even to the point of caring about our growling stomachs. The Psalmist wrote, "The LORD is merciful and gracious, slow to anger, and abounding in mercy," Psalm 103:8.

Read Matthew 14:14. "And when Jesus went out He saw a great multitude; and *He was moved with compassion* for them, and healed their sick." Notice, Jesus had compassion on the crowds before even one person said, "Jesus, I'm sick," or, "Jesus, I'm hungry."

Why should God, being God, care about such matters; about whether we eat or get sick or arrive home safely? Because compassion is a part of God's nature. Don't think of Christ's miracles merely as acts of great power, but also as acts of great compassion.

Indeed, the great compassion of God is seen in this, that He gives us what we do not deserve: forgiveness, daily bread, eternal life.

## The Savior's Involvement

Matthew 14:13-21 is often called the *Feeding of the Five Thousand.* Including women and children, however, the number was perhaps more like thirty thousand. One look at such a crowd, and Jesus could have easily turned away. But He didn't. Instead, His great compassion moved Him to great action. He fed each man, woman, and child.

What better demonstrates God's involvement in our daily lives than the incarnation of Jesus Christ, His coming to be with us and one of us? What better demonstrates God's involvement in even the worst of our circumstances than the sacrifice of Christ to atone for our sins? And if Jesus willingly laid down His life for us, will He begrudge us a change of clothes or a loaf of bread? Of course not.

## The Savior's Power

Jesus is God. Jesus has all power. Jesus can do anything. These are obvious lessons from the *Feeding of the Five Thousand*. I'd like to see even one so-called faith healer feed thirty thousand people from five loaves of bread and two small fish—or for that matter, walk on water or change water into wine or raise the dead at the nearest funeral home. Many, if not most, are outright charlatans who won't even make an appearance without television cameras, applause, and sizeable donations.

Jesus has the power; we don't. You and I desperately need to learn this lesson. So did the Lord's original disciples. They were the ones who brought meal-time to Jesus' attention. According to Matthew 14:15, "When it was evening, His disciples came to Him, saying, 'This is a deserted place, and the hour is already late. Send the multitudes away, that they may go into the villages and buy themselves food.'" What was the Savior's response? "You give them something to eat," Matthew 14:16.

I would have enjoyed seeing the look on the disciples' faces at that moment. Most of us panic when a few friends or relatives arrive unannounced for dinner. Try thirty thousand. Perhaps the disciples looked at each other helplessly, or checked their pockets for loose change, or wondered if they had misunderstood Jesus.

The real question is, why did Jesus give His disciples such an impossible task? Because He knew the disciples could not feed the multitudes, and He wanted them to realize that He could.

Amazingly, none of the disciples retained this lesson. Not

long afterwards, when faced with a similar impossibility at the *Feeding of the Four Thousand*, the disciples asked Jesus, "Where could we get enough bread in the wilderness to fill such a great multitude?" Matthew 15:33.

SIGH.

But perhaps we can forgive the disciples, knowing that we have all done the same. How many times has God delivered us from heartache, trouble, pain, loss, and guilt; yet, we still doubt His power to deliver us from future problems?

SIGH AGAIN.

Jesus said in Matthew 28:18, "All authority has been given to Me in heaven and on earth." All authority. All power. This means that *He* is the one who miraculously provides the meal. All we do is collect the leftovers.

**The Savior's Generosity**

The Lord blesses us so richly that He always leaves us leftovers. As in Matthew 14:20, "So they all ate and were filled, and they took up twelve baskets full of the fragments that remained." Or as in John 1:16, "And of His fullness we have all received, and grace for grace."

When facing hardship and heartache, remember this Miraculous Meal. Remember the Savior's compassion, involvement, power, and the generosity with which He laid down His life and daily provides for our needs.

# Ambassadors for Christ

2 Corinthians 5:18-6:2

*If the president of the United States appointed us to serve as U.S. ambassadors, we would be honored beyond description. Do we feel the same excitement for our roles as ambassadors for Christ?*

Imagine receiving a phone call from the President of the United States. "I'm calling," he explains, "because I have chosen *you* to serve as a U.S. ambassador." How would you feel? Wouldn't you be honored? Wouldn't you be confident, knowing that you were backed by the authority of the most powerful nation on earth? Wouldn't you work tirelessly and diligently, given the importance of your position? In fact, wouldn't your ambassadorship profoundly impact many areas of your life—your thoughts, words, and actions?

"Well, I suppose," you might say. "But this is just imagining, right? I will never be a U.S. ambassador." No, perhaps not. What you may not realize, however, is that you have already been appointed to a far greater ambassadorship by a far greater authority than the President of the United States. You are an ambassador for Christ. As the apostle Paul wrote, "Now then, we are ambassadors for Christ," 2 Corinthians 5:20. "We," he said. Not merely some. Not merely the apostles. Not merely pastors and teachers. All Christians. If you are a believer in Jesus Christ, you are also an ambassador for Jesus Christ.

## The Appointment

In reality, if the President of the United States called any one of us to serve as *his* ambassador, we would be honored beyond description. But do we have the same excitement and enthusiasm for our roles as ambassadors for Christ? How many of our friends, coworkers, or even next-door neighbors know that we are Christians?

Paul wrote in 2 Corinthians 5:18, "Now all things are of God, who has reconciled us to Himself through Jesus Christ, and has given us the ministry of reconciliation." Contemplate this great truth: Almighty God chose you to serve as Christ's ambassador. Shouldn't this fill you with joy, honor, and a deep sense of gratitude?

Consequently, when you are about to share God's Word with someone; or when you are reaching for a doorbell while canvassing a neighborhood, remind yourself, "I am an ambassador for Jesus Christ! God appointed me to represent Him!"

### The Message

Throughout history, the primary role of an ambassador has always been to faithfully represent the one who sent him. In antiquity, the relationship between an ambassador and his king was so close that to insult the ambassador was to insult the king and even to invite a war.

Of course, to faithfully represent his king, an ambassador had to faithfully convey the king's words and will, not his own. For an ambassador to change the king's message in any way, for any reason—adding or subtracting words, removing threats or promises, using half-truths instead of the whole truth—was in no way representing the king. And if this is true of earthly kings, it is far truer of the King of Kings, Almighty God.

The Bible is God's message to the world, the message He gave His ambassadors to share. And *no one* has the right to change the King's message. Yet, sadly and shamefully, we see this happening—especially in churches where the emphasis is more on packed pews than on proclaiming the Bible in its truth and entirety. They don't seem to realize that to challenge any part of God's Word is to challenge the whole. How can one truly be an ambassador for Christ without faithfully proclaiming the words and will of Christ?

"Your word is truth," said Jesus in John 17:17. And praise God that His Word is truth; because in it we find a glorious message for ourselves, our loved ones, and the whole world. Paul referred to this message as "the word of reconciliation," 2 Corinthians 5:19. The term *reconciliation* is from the Latin *reconciliare*, which literally means "to make friendly again."

How did God reconcile the sinful world to Himself? Did He change His view on sin? No. God does not change. A changeable God is no God at all. Then, did we change? Did we suddenly become less sinful and more desirable? Again, no. According to Scripture, "all have sinned and fall short of the glory of God," Romans 3:23.

How then did God reconcile the world to Himself? Wonder of wonders, grace beyond grace, He punished His own Son, Jesus Christ, instead of punishing us. As Paul wrote in 2 Corinthians 5:21, God "made Him who knew no sin to be sin for us, that we might become the righteousness of God in Him." This is the glorious message of reconciliation that God has entrusted to us as Christ's ambassadors; a message of joy, hope, and salvation intended for all Mankind.

**The Urgency**

The first month I moved to Fort Myers, Florida, I noticed a middle-aged woman sitting on a green metal bench outside of a Publix Supermarket. Day after day, hour after hour, the same woman, the same bench, the same blistering sun; the same chain-smoking between coughing fits and sips of water.

The woman wasn't homeless, or so I was told by a Publix employee. "I don't know her name," said the employee, "but she lives in the apartments across the street. She comes here every day, and has for a long while. I guess she's lonely. Sad, really."

As the months passed, every time I went to Publix I looked for the woman. Every time I told myself, "Today I will stop to say hello, or to see if she needs anything, or even to invite her to church." But something always intervened. Somehow, the shopping list became more important than that poor woman. And then one day, she was gone. Just gone. I never saw her again.

I didn't know that woman. But I do know this about her: God loved her. God redeemed her. God reconciled her to Himself in Jesus Christ. Only, I wonder if *she* knew that? I wonder why, as an ambassador for Jesus Christ, I didn't make the time to tell her?

Paul wrote, "Behold, NOW is the accepted time; behold, NOW is the day of salvation," 2 Corinthians 6:2.

# An Unexpected Ending

Luke 18:9-14

*Many expected God to praise the Pharisee and condemn the tax collector. Only, that's not what happened.*

Have you ever read a novel with a completely unexpected ending, an ending that left you stunned, shaking your head, and thinking, "I never saw that coming"?

Perhaps the people who heard Jesus tell the *Parable of the Pharisee and Tax Collector* felt exactly the same. Most were likely Pharisees, as Luke described them, "some who trusted in themselves that they were righteous, and despised others," Luke 18:9. As such, they were no doubt thrilled with the premise of the parable: Two men praying in the temple, one a Pharisee, the other a tax collector. From their perspective, any story about a Pharisee and a tax collector would have to be a good story with a good ending, in which the Pharisee was praised and the tax collector was condemned.

Only that's not how the parable ended.

According to Jesus, the tax collector "went down to his house justified," Luke 18:14. And at this, the listeners were stunned, disappointed, even angry. "What?" they thought. "How could this be? This was not the ending we expected." Of course they did not expect this ending, because they did not expect God to reject the religious Pharisee and to forgive the sinful tax collector. But He did.

God's ways are not our ways. And His way to salvation is very different from Man's way. In the unexpected ending of His parable, Jesus taught that salvation is not based on who we are, but on Who God is—not on our works, but on God's redemptive work in Jesus Christ.

**Not Us, But Him**

Pharisees were the religious elite in Israel: church-goers, alms-givers, law-keepers, concerned about every "jot and tittle" of the Mosaic Law, but often ignoring its intent and essence, eager to strain out a gnat while swallowing a camel.

The Pharisees viewed themselves as a "cut above the rest," as implied by the name Pharisee itself—from the Hebrew word *PARASH*, meaning "separated one." As the Pharisee said in the parable, "God, I thank You that I am not like other men," Luke 18:11.

If the Pharisee represented society's best, the tax collector represented the worst. Most tax collectors in Judea were Jews employed by the Roman government, and were therefore viewed as collaborators, traitors, and even idolaters. At the time of Jesus, tax collectors were permitted to use any method they chose, and to collect any amount they desired, as long as the Roman government received its share. Abuse was rampant.

Simply put, the Pharisee in the parable was the *good guy*, and the tax collector was the *bad guy*. Yet, it was the latter, not the former, who went home justified. Why? God's definition of good is very different from Man's definition. And when it comes to salvation, Man's good is never good enough. As the psalmist wrote: "There is none who does good, no, not one," Psalm 14:3. No, not even a Pharisee.

Our salvation is not based on who we are, but on Who God is. The tax collector in the parable understood this while, ironically, the religious Pharisee did not. The Pharisee expected God to save him because he was a good person. The tax collector believed God would save him despite his having been a bad person. Why? Because He knew who God is; the gracious, merciful God who forgives even the worst of sinners when they turn to Him in humility, repentance, and faith.

## Not Our Works, But His

According to one source, there are more than 4,200 religions in the world today. Yet, of all these religions, only one teaches that Man cannot save himself, that salvation is not by works but by grace, not by doing but by simply believing in Jesus Christ as Lord and Savior. That one religion, of course, is Christianity as taught by the Bible.

Salvation by works makes perfect sense to human reason and human nature. As human beings, we must work for everything else—work to eat, work to pay bills, work to enrich a troubled marriage. "Hi-ho, hi-ho, it's off to work we go."

So, why can't our good works justify us before God? Because we are sinful by nature. Because, as Isaiah wrote, "But we are all like an unclean thing, and all our righteousnesses are like filthy rags," Isaiah 64:6.

Salvation by works was the approach of the Pharisee. Standing in the bright spotlight of self-righteousness, he boasted about his good works. "I fast twice a week," he said. "I give tithes of all that I possess," Luke 18:12. Admirable? Yes, but not "savable"; that is, not able to save. For despite all his good deeds, the Pharisee did not go home justified before God; the tax collector did. An unexpected ending.

In Christ's remarkable parable, the Pharisee is not only an example of how our good character can never be good enough to save us; but also how our good works—regardless of quantity or quality—can never justify us before Almighty God. As Paul wrote to the Galatians: "We who are Jews by nature, and not sinners of the Gentiles, knowing that a man is not justified by the works of the law but by faith in Jesus Christ, even we have believed in Christ Jesus, that we might be justified by faith in Christ and not by the works of the law; for by the works of the law no flesh shall be justified," Galatians 2:15-16.

So, through faith in Christ, we poor sinners also have an unexpected ending, a glorious ending that we had no right or reason to expect: the forgiveness of sins and eternal salvation.

# Beneath the Juniper Tree

1 Kings 19:1-9

*Elijah was a great prophet. Yet, this same prophet ran for his life, slumped down beneath a juniper tree, and prayed for death.*

Have you ever wanted to give up? If so, you're not alone. At one point in his life, a very *low* point, the prophet Elijah felt exactly the same. Fleeing into the desert, he slumped beneath a juniper tree and begged God to end his life. "Now, LORD," he said, "take my life, for I am no better than my fathers," 1 Kings 19:4.

How could Elijah sink into such despair? He was a prophet of God. His very name expressed confidence in the Almighty. Elijah, *ELIYAH* in Hebrew, means "My God is Jehovah." In the name and power of Jehovah, Elijah fiercely opposed the wickedness of King Ahab and Queen Jezebel. At God's command, he prayed for drought, and drought came. He prayed for rain, and rain fell.

During the drought, Elijah was fed by ravens at the Brook of Cherith; and later, he was fed by a widow in Zarephath, Phoenicia. As long as he remained in the widow's home, a period of at least two years, her handful of flour and few drops of olive oil never ran out. Elijah even raised the widow's son from the dead.

Yet, this same prophet ran for his life, then prayed for death at a juniper tree in the desert. More remarkable still, Elijah's fear and depression came shortly after one of his greatest victories—his triumph over the eight hundred and fifty prophets of Baal and Asherah on Mount Carmel.

With such a demonstration of God's power and presence, surely Elijah would have no fears and no doubts amid future problems. Only this is not what happened. Suddenly, almost inexplicably, after one threat from Queen Jezebel, Elijah fled from Mount Carmel to Beersheba, a distance of one hundred and fifty miles. Fled into the desert. Fled to a juniper tree, where he begged God to end his miserable existence. Afterwards, he fled to a cave on Mount Horeb, also known as Mount Sinai. Why?

Elijah was a great prophet, but he was also a human being with human weaknesses and human frailties. James wrote, "Elijah was a man with a nature like ours," James 5:17. Frankly, I find this comforting—not Elijah's weakness, but his humanity—the fact that he needed God as much as we do.

When things did not go as Elijah expected, he gave up. He thought "what's the use?" But we do the same, don't we? One comment from Queen Jezebel terrified Elijah. One comment from a doctor, "It's cancer," or from a spouse, "I want a divorce," or from an employer, "You're fired," can terrify us, too. So, when we find ourselves slumped beneath our own juniper tree, what should we do?

## Remember What God Has Done

When depressed, did Elijah remember what God had done for him in the past? I don't know. If he did remember, he may have brushed the past aside as irrelevant to his personal circumstances. Regardless, while we hurry to criticize Elijah, are we not like him in this regard, too? In the middle of some crisis, some need, have we not forgotten God's past dealings with us, or considered His past dealings irrelevant to our current circumstances? As a result, we run. We hide. We slump beneath our juniper tree, wondering who will help us while insisting no one can.

When lying beneath our juniper tree, we should be asking, "Has God ever failed me in the past? Has there been one day when God has not fed or clothed me, provided for me, or kept my heart beating the 115,200 times it beats each day? And if things have not gone as I expected, hasn't God always had a purpose in this, too—whether saving me from my own foolishness, or giving me a far greater resolution than I could have imagined for myself? So, am I going to lie here beneath this juniper tree, feeling sorry for myself? Or am I going to get up, brush myself off, and live the confident, triumphant life God gave me in Jesus Christ?"

In fact, more than anything else, we should remember what God has done for us in Jesus Christ. If God did not withhold the life of His own Son, but sacrificed Him to atone for our sins, will He withhold any other blessings from us: a loaf of bread, change of clothes, source of income, happy marriage? No. Focusing on God's past dealings with us will empower us to stop asking "what if" and to start saying "no matter what."

## Remember to Eat

As Elijah lay beneath his juniper tree, an angel of the LORD told him, "Arise and eat, because the journey is too great for you," 1 Kings 19:7. So, Elijah ate the food God provided; and strengthened by it, he was empowered to complete his journey from the juniper tree to Mount Sinai.

Surely there is a lesson here for us. When depressed, people often stay away from church. They say, "I just don't feel like moving, listening, praying, singing, or being around other people." While this is understandable, it is not advisable. Staying away from church only feeds our depression, not our faith. Indeed, when we stay away from the Word of God, we are staying away from that which the Savior called "the one thing needed," and what Paul described as "the power of God for salvation."

If you are depressed, you absolutely need to feed on God's Word. So, leave your juniper tree and go to church. And if you can't leave your juniper tree, take it with you. Overcome it with another tree: the tree on which Jesus died to save you from your sins.

## Remember That God Is Working

Elijah's basic premise was "LORD, I did my part, but You failed to do Yours." Or in Elijah's own words, "I have been very zealous for the LORD God of hosts; for the children of Israel have forsaken Your covenant, torn down Your altars, and killed Your prophets with the sword. I alone am left; and they seek to take my life," 1 Kings 19:10.

What was wrong with Elijah's assessment? It wasn't factual. Elijah was not the only prophet of God remaining in Israel. According to 1 Kings 18, a man named Obadiah had hidden one hundred prophets of God in caves. Elijah knew this, but in his depression, he may have felt alone—the only person living with his kind of problems.

But Elijah was wrong about something else, too. Unknown to him, even when everything and everyone seemed to be out of control, God was quietly working through the still, small voice of the gospel, accomplishing His great purposes.

And so God told a surprised Elijah, "Yet I have reserved seven thousand in Israel, all whose knees have not bowed to Baal, and every mouth that has not kissed him," 1 Kings 19:18. In other words, there is never a time when we have a valid reason for sitting beneath a juniper tree, thinking, "Sharing God's word with others is not worth the effort." It is worth the effort, because Almighty God is always working through His Word; always building His Church; always controlling His world; always accomplishing His great purposes for our lives.

# By Faith

Habakkuk 1:1-3; 2:1-4

*Amid all the turmoil of Habakkuk's world, nation, life, and calling, he brought his questions to God. God answered, and His answer was "by faith."*

Little is known of Habakkuk's life. He was a prophet of God, and perhaps a priest or Levite in the temple at Jerusalem. The third and final chapter of his brief book was meant to be set to music and used in public worship. "To the Chief Musician," he wrote in 3:19. "With my stringed instruments."

More is known about when and why Habakkuk prophesied. Like his contemporaries, the prophets Jeremiah and Zephaniah, Habakkuk was sent to the southern kingdom of Judah to warns its inhabitants of impending judgment.

Conditions in Judah at that time were deplorable. Habakkuk described them this way: "For plundering and violence are before me; there is strife, and contention arises. Therefore the law is powerless, and justice never goes forth. For the wicked surround the righteous; therefore perverse judgment proceeds," 1:3b-4.

One of the most endearing aspects of the Book of Habakkuk is the personal dialogue between the perplexed prophet and his loving God. To paraphrase their conversation: Habakkuk asks, "God, why are so many bad things happening? Why aren't You acting?" God answers, "I am acting, but in a way you did not expect." And in the middle of this conversation lies one of the grandest, most important verses in the Bible, spoken by God Himself: "But the just shall live by his faith," 2:4.

Ultimately, everything about the Christian life—from conversion to conclusion, forgiveness to salvation, daily bread to eternal life, obstacles to accomplishments, marriage to ministry—is a matter of faith, of trusting God. And at its simplest, faith is taking God at His word. As was said of Abraham: "He did not waver at the promise of God through unbelief, but was strengthened in faith, giving glory to God, and being fully convinced that what He had promised He was also able to perform," Romans 4:20-21.

Amid the turmoil and complexities of his world, nation, life, and calling, Habakkuk brought his questions to God. And God answered them. And the essence of God's answer was "Trust Me, Habakkuk." God says the same to us. "Trust Me. Have faith in Me. You know Who I am, what I am like, what I can do, and what I have done to redeem you."

## Saved by Faith

People ask important questions every day. "What time is it?" "When will you be home?" "Is your seatbelt fastened?" "Is dinner ready?" "Do you love me?" Yet, the most important question we can ever ask is "How am I saved?" And if this seems a trivial question, try asking it on your deathbed. Try answering it apart from the Word of God. Try finding the certainty of salvation in your own merit or good deeds, through money in the bank or awards on the shelf. It cannot be done.

Some days we feel wonderful, skipping along with joy in our hearts and *Amazing Grace* on our lips. But on other days we feel like the tax collector who said, "God, be merciful to me a sinner," Luke 18:13; or like the apostle Paul who said, "Christ Jesus came into the world to save sinners, of whom I am chief," 1 Timothy 1:15.

If you have never experienced the crushing weight of sin and guilt, you will. And when you do, would you like to hear from God, "Sorry, I am all out of forgiveness; come back tomorrow," or perhaps, "Go keep the Ten Commandments perfectly, and then we'll talk"?

If God's plan for salvation were human works, the only

certainty we could have would be the certainty of being eternally lost and eternally punished. As the psalmist wrote: "If You, LORD, should mark iniquities, O Lord, who could stand? But there is forgiveness with You, that You may be feared," Psalm 130:3-4.

The Bible repeatedly teaches that salvation is not by doing but by believing; that is, by faith in Jesus Christ as Lord and Savior. "Therefore," Paul wrote in Romans 5:1, "having been justified by faith, we have peace with God through our Lord Jesus Christ."

There may be Sundays when we go to church, open the bulletin, read the sermon title, and think, "I wish I could hear something other than the same old gospel truths: sin, salvation, forgiveness, grace, faith in Christ. I know all these things." Instead of expressing frustration, however, we should express thanks to God that His great gospel truths never change; that whether life or death, ups or downs, riches or poverty, health or sickness, youth or age—when we have Jesus Christ by faith, we have all that we need for time and eternity.

## Living by Faith

However, the great truth of "by faith" does not apply only to eternal life, but equally to daily life. This is the plain and simple meaning of the verse "the just shall live by his faith," Habakkuk 2:4.

When suffering illness, we live by faith that God will take care of us. When struggling with finances, we live by faith that God will provide for us. When endeavoring to repair a troubled marriage or find the strength to forgive another person, we live by faith that God will empower us.

Habakkuk wrote his book more than 2,600 years ago. Yet, his opening words have a very modern ring: "For plundering and violence are before me; there is strife, and contention arises," 1:3. While the prophet was talking about the kingdom of Judah, he could have easily been talking about the United

States of America.

"Why do You show me iniquity, and cause me to see trouble?" Habakkuk asked God in 1:3. We ask the same question, don't we? Who is in charge of the world, our national affairs, our personal lives? Anyone?

Yet, Someone is in charge. And His name is Jesus Christ. And He has all power in heaven and on earth. And that which is happening in the world today is by His consent or His design. We don't see this with our eyes. But we see it clearly by faith.

# Case Number J81-11

John 8:1-11

*Jesus Christ, the only One in court that day Who had a right to throw a stone, instead offered a condemned woman love, mercy, and forgiveness.*

I've come to think of it as Case Number J81-11, that is, John 8:1-11, the account of a woman caught in the act of adultery, rushed from the bedroom to the courtroom by religious authorities, and condemned to death. In reality, as frightened and distraught as the woman was, she may have been only incidental to the case—merely a pawn used by the plaintiffs, the scribes and Pharisees, to find a basis to discredit Jesus.

Under the Mosaic Law, both the adulterer and the adulteress were to be put to death. Yet, in Case Number J81-11, only the adulteress was present in court. How could this be when she was caught in the very act of adultery? Where was the man who was caught in the same act? Some believe the man was part of the plot. Once his part was accomplished, he was set free.

If true, consider the implications. Consider that the holier-than-thou religious leaders in Jerusalem may have orchestrated an act of adultery simply to ensnare Jesus. They told Jesus, "Now Moses, in the law, commanded us that such should be stoned. But what do You say?" John 8:5. As John explained, "This they said, testing Him, that they might have something of which to accuse Him," John 8:6.

What did Jesus do? He initially ignored them. Instead of answering, He stooped down and wrote on the ground. When the plaintiffs persisted in questioning Him, He stood, spoke a single sentence, knelt down again, and continued writing. This is what Jesus told them: "He who is without sin among you, let him throw a stone at her first," John 8:7. "Then those who heard it, being convicted by their conscience, went out one by one, beginning with the oldest even to the last. And Jesus was left alone, and the woman standing in the midst," John 8:9.

And then the most touching scene of all; a scene I can barely read without feeling a swell of emotion. Jesus Christ, the Son of God, the Creator of the universe—the only One in court that day who had the right to throw a stone—instead, offered the condemned woman love, mercy, and forgiveness; a woman who had been crushed by the reality of her sin and the enormity of her guilt.

"Woman," asked Jesus, "where are those accusers of yours? Has no one condemned you?" John 8:10. She replied, "No one, Lord." And Jesus said, "Neither do I condemn you; go and sin no more," John 8:11.

Why does this case, Case Number J81-11, so comfort and inspire us? Is it simply that the self-righteous scribes and Pharisees failed in their plot to discredit Jesus? Is it simply that the accusers in the crowd dropped the case and dropped the stones and walked away? Is it simply the vivid image of the woman caught in the very act of adultery—ashamed, embarrassed, bereft of dignity and hope, perhaps cringing on the ground with tears streaking the dust on her face? These are all important aspects of the case, but not the most important aspect.

No, the most important aspect of Case Number J81-11 is this: we have all been like that woman. We have all been "caught in the act" of sinning against God. And we have all been shown the same undeserved love, mercy, and forgiveness of God in Jesus Christ.

If we do not see ourselves as sinful, then we do not understand the law of God any better than the scribes and Pharisees—and they were the legal experts. And if we insist on throwing stones at contrite sinners who have repented of their sins and asked for forgiveness, then we do not understand the gospel of God either—or how much we ourselves have been forgiven.

Scripture teaches the difference between law and gospel not only in proof passages. It also teaches this important difference within the context of real flesh and blood, real human problems, and real human failings—like Case Number J81-11, where the law showed an adulterous woman her sin; and the gospel liberated her with the blessed reality: "Neither do I condemn you; go and sin no more."

# Characteristics of a Gospel Ministry

## Luke 15

*In the parables of Luke 15, so richly colored with Christ's own ministry, we learn how we, too, are to seek the lost.*

Jesus often told parables. A parable was not only an effective teaching device; it was also a means through which Jesus taught higher spiritual truths about the kingdom of God.

This is certainly true of the parables of Luke 15. The images are beautiful in and of themselves: the shepherd who searches for one lost sheep, the woman who scours her house to find one lost coin, and the father who runs to embrace his lost son.

Yet, along with these cherished images, we also see the greater realities of Jesus the Good Shepherd, Who came to seek and to save us. We see the heavenly Father, Who welcomes us home with open arms of forgiveness when we turn to Him in repentance and faith. Indeed, in the three lost-and-found parables of Luke 15, so richly colored by Christ's own ministry, we also learn how we, too, are to seek the lost.

### A Committed Ministry

The first characteristic of a gospel ministry is personal commitment. Do we have it? The shepherd and the woman in the parables certainly did. When the shepherd realized that one sheep was missing, he did not wait for a more convenient time. He immediately went and with singleness of purpose sought that lost sheep.

When the woman realized one coin was missing, she didn't search indifferently, thinking, "It's only one coin."

Instead, she searched diligently. In fact, the Greek verbs used to describe this woman's actions are all in the present tense, ongoing and relentless. She keeps the lamp lit. She continues to sweep, clean, and scour. She continues searching in dark corners, under sofa cushions, and the unlikeliest of places, until her one lost coin is found.

And nowhere is this type of ongoing action and relentless commitment better exemplified than in the personal ministry of our Lord Jesus Christ—of Whom we read in Matthew 9: "Then Jesus went about all the cities and villages, teaching in their synagogues, preaching the gospel of the kingdom, and healing every sickness and every disease among the people. But when He saw the multitudes, He was moved with compassion for them, because they were weary and scattered, like sheep having no shepherd."

Yes, Jesus always welcomed the multitudes who came to Him. But first and foremost, He went to them. His was a ministry of personal commitment and personal involvement. Ours must be too.

### An Urgent Ministry

The second characteristic of a gospel ministry is a sense of urgency. Do we have it? Like the lost sheep, lost coin, and lost son in Luke 15, there are countless lost people in this world—people without hope because they are without God. And tragically, they will be lost eternally, unless they come to embrace Christ as Lord and Savior. This is the reason for the urgency.

Yet, the same Bible that states we are lost by nature also assures us that we will never be lost if we are in Christ by faith. "For God so loved the world that He gave His only begotten Son, that whoever believes in Him should not perish but have everlasting life," John 3:16. In this cherished Bible verse, the Greek word translated as "perish" is the same word translated as "lost" in Luke 15. When we believe in God's one and only Son, we will not be lost, but have eternal life.

## A Welcoming Ministry

The third characteristic of a gospel ministry is a joyful, welcoming spirit. Do we have it? The father in the parables of Luke 15 surely did. When he saw his lost son in the distance, he ran to embrace him with outstretched arms, teary eyes, perhaps nearly tripping in his haste. He forgave his prodigal son, celebrated his return, and welcomed him home. Our heavenly Father does the same when any sinner comes to his senses and comes home through Christ.

When the religious leaders of Israel saw Jesus forgiving, healing, and welcoming sinners, they were incensed. "This Man receives sinners and eats with them," they accused in Luke 15:2. Ironically, their accusation was true; and is, in fact, the very heart of the gospel message: "The Son of Man has come to seek and to save that which was lost," Luke 19:10.

## A Grateful Ministry

The fourth characteristic of a gospel ministry is gratitude. Do we have it? At times, we have all been like the prodigal son, haven't we? Running away from our heavenly Father. Ignoring His word. Caring more about want than need. Pursuing foolish ambitions that led to the same pigpen and same empty husks. And yet, when we turn to God in repentance, He always welcomes us home. He runs to meet us. He embraces us despite the pig-stink on our clothes. He celebrates our return.

This is where true gospel outreach begins; not in church or seminary, but in a heart bursting with personal gratitude for God's grace in Jesus Christ. "This is a faithful saying," Paul wrote in 1 Timothy 1:15, "and worthy of all acceptance, that Christ Jesus came into the world to save sinners, of whom I am chief."

It was this personal gratitude that compelled Paul to share the gospel everywhere and with everyone.

# Christmas Is About

Titus 2:11-14

*Christmas has nothing to do with what we deserve, and everything to do with what we don't deserve: forgiveness and salvation through Jesus Christ.*

You've likely seen the holiday classic *A Charlie Brown Christmas*. In it Charlie Brown agonizes over the true meaning of Christmas. "I think something must be wrong with me," he tells Linus. "Christmas is coming, but I'm not happy. I don't feel the way I'm supposed to feel."

To make matters worse, many in the Peanuts Gang have a strictly commercial view of Christmas. Lucy wants real estate. Sally wants cash, preferably tens and twenties. Snoopy wants to organize a neighborhood Christmas lights contest, with a cash award going to the winner. His invitation reads: "Come see what Christmas is all about. Money. Money. Money."

Frustrated, Charlie Brown cries out, "Does anyone know what Christmas is all about?" We, too, may ask this question when preparing for the Christmas Season. And if the preparations don't distract us from the true meaning of Christmas, personal circumstances often do: sickness, debt, the loss of a loved one.

Soon enough, we may find ourselves lamenting with Charlie Brown, "Christmas is coming, but I'm not happy. I don't feel the way I'm supposed to feel." And yet, our feelings are not meant to determine Christmas. The facts of Christmas are meant to determine our feelings. What are the facts?

**Christmas Is about God's Faithfulness**

Admittedly, the faithfulness of God is not specifically mentioned in Titus 2:11-14; but it is certainly implied. When

Paul writes, "For the grace of God that brings salvation has appeared to all men," he is referring to the appearance of Jesus Christ: His birth in Bethlehem, His ministry, miracles, teaching, suffering, atoning death and resurrection—all that Jesus did to accomplish our eternal salvation. Yet, the only reason Christ appeared that First Christmas was that God was faithful in keeping His promise to send a Savior.

Human promises roll off human lips with relative ease; and, despite best intentions, frequently fail. But not so with the promises of Almighty God. By some estimates, more than three hundred Old Testament prophecies or promises were fulfilled with the coming of Christ. And God fulfilled each one because God is faithful.

Has God promised to save you? He will. Has God promised to deliver you safely from this life to the next? He will. Has God promised to forgive you whenever you turn to Him in repentance and faith? He will. Has God promised to enrich your marriage, prosper your ministry, and provide for all your needs? He will. And Christmas is the proof.

## Christmas Is about God's Grace

Paul wrote of "the grace of God that brings salvation." The New Testament uses the word *grace* one hundred and fifty-six times, referring to such blessings as standing in grace, Romans 5:2; living under grace, Romans 6:14; being chosen by grace, Romans 11:5; having gifts of grace, Romans 12:6; being called by grace, Galatians 1:6; being forgiven through the riches of God's grace, Ephesians 1:7; and being saved by grace, Ephesians 2:8-9.

But what is grace? Simply put, grace is God's undeserved love, kindness, and goodwill expressed in Christ Jesus—the very Christmas blessings proclaimed to shepherds as they watched their flocks by night: "Glory to God in the highest, and on earth peace, goodwill toward men," Luke 2:14.

Consequently, Christmas has nothing to do with what we deserve, and everything to do with what we do not deserve;

namely, forgiveness and salvation through Christ.

## Christmas Is about Change

Some years ago, I attended a Christmas concert. During various readings and Christmas hymns, a video began to play on a large screen. The video was of a little baby, wrapped in swaddling clothes, lying in a manger, moving his tiny fingers and toes while smiling.

For one instant, the baby turned his head and looked at the audience with wondrously brown eyes. And suddenly, the meaning of Christmas swept over me anew. God, the almighty God, came to us just like that little baby, wiggling His toes and fingers, and smiling at us in wonder.

Think about John's words in the first chapter of his gospel: "And the Word became flesh and dwelt among us," John 1:14. What a remarkable, miraculous sentence! Not only does the Gospel tell us about Jesus; Jesus Himself is the Gospel—the Good News Who came to us in flesh and blood. God didn't merely send us inspired writings and letters, prophets and apostles. When He wanted to show us the full extent of His love, God sent His one and only Son. How can we know that and not be changed?

This is why Paul wrote, "For the grace of God that brings salvation has appeared to all men, teaching us that, denying ungodliness and worldly lusts, we should live soberly, righteously, and godly in the present age, looking for the blessed hope and glorious appearing of our great God and Savior Jesus Christ, who gave Himself for us, that He might redeem us from every lawless deed and purify for Himself His own special people, zealous for good works," Titus 2:11-14.

# Compelled to Preach

## 1 Corinthians 9:16

*The apostle Paul made three extensive missionary journeys, and by some estimates traveled more than twenty-five thousand miles. What compelled him to travel so far and to endure so much to preach the gospel?*

For nearly thirty years, the apostle Paul preached the gospel of Christ to kings and commoners, Jews and Gentiles, men and women, young and old. During that time, he made three extensive missionary journeys, and by some estimates traveled more than twenty-five thousand miles. Along the way, he endured fierce opposition and suffered many hardships: hunger, thirst, cold, nakedness, sleeplessness, beatings, betrayal, stoning, persecution; and all this while struggling with that mysterious "thorn in the flesh."

Surely, all of us have marveled at Paul's tireless commitment to preaching the gospel. "Necessity is laid on me," he said. But what was that necessity? What compelled Paul to travel so far and to endure so much to preach the gospel?

## The Divine Call

Paul was compelled to preach by his divine call; by the fact that God had chosen him, privileged him, and called him to be an apostle of Jesus Christ. Remember, ministry was not Paul's chosen profession. Before his conversion on the road to Damascus, Paul was a persecutor and prosecutor. He was not a preacher. The fact that Saul of Tarsus became Paul the Apostle was due solely to God's design and call, a fact to which Paul attested in nine of his thirteen epistles, including the introduction to First Corinthians: "Paul, called to be an apostle of Jesus Christ through the will of God."

You may not be an apostle like Paul. Nevertheless, God has called you to share the gospel with others. Simon Peter wrote, "But you are a chosen generation, a royal priesthood, a holy nation, His own special people, that you may proclaim the praises of Him who called you out of darkness into His marvelous light," 1 Peter 2:9. If we recognize this call to share Christ as a privilege instead of a chore, we, too, will say with Paul, "For necessity is laid upon me; yes, woe is me if I do not preach the gospel!"

## The Inner Conviction

Paul was compelled to preach the gospel not from an outer coercion, but from an inner conviction worked by the Spirit of God. All those truly called into the public ministry feel this same inner conviction. It's what leads them to the seminary. It's what compels them to go on preaching and teaching and ministering despite personal or congregational circumstances.

However, in a more general sense, outside of the public ministry, all Christians speak about Christ from a deep, inner conviction worked by the Holy Spirit. And that deep inner conviction is faith. Paul wrote in 2 Corinthians 4:13, "And since we have the same spirit of faith, according to what is written, 'I believed and therefore I spoke,' we also believe and therefore speak."

## The Urgency

Paul was compelled to preach the gospel because there is no other way for lost sinners to be saved. This is what led him to write, "I have become all things to all men, that I might by all means save some. Now this I do for the gospel's sake, that I may be partaker of it with you," 1 Corinthians 9:22-23.

Saving others is what compelled Paul. Saving others is what should compel us—not statistics, not increasing Sunday attendance, not building massive cathedrals. We are compelled to preach the gospel, because it alone "is the power of God to salvation for everyone who believes," Romans 1:16.

## The Humble Gratitude

Paul was compelled to preach the gospel because of the same blessings the gospel brought to him. "Now this I do for the gospel's sake, that I may be partaker of it with you," he said. Finally, it is a deep, personal appreciation of what Jesus Christ has done for each of us that, above all else, compels us to preach Jesus Christ to others.

Paul's humble gratitude for his salvation and calling is evident in his words to Timothy, "And I thank Christ Jesus our Lord who has enabled me, because He counted me faithful, putting me into the ministry, although I was formerly a blasphemer, a persecutor, and an insolent man; but I obtained mercy because I did it ignorantly in unbelief. And the grace of our Lord was exceedingly abundant, with faith and love which are in Christ Jesus. This is a faithful saying and worthy of all acceptance, that Christ Jesus came into the world to save sinners, of whom I am chief," 1 Timothy 1:12-15.

# Dollars and Sense

Mark 10:17-27

*In Scripture, God neither commends nor condemns wealth. But He repeatedly warns us of its limitations and dangers.*

It was Vacation Bible School, and the children were participating in a special offering. I was the one holding the collection plate. When I came to one small boy, he reached into his pocket, rooted, produced a paper clip and stick of gum, but no offering. To his credit, however, he kept digging. Not wishing to embarrass the boy, I looked away. And precisely then, he dropped a coin into the plate.

Not knowing this, I continued to wait by his pew. I even encouraged the boy, saying, "Take your time. It's okay." Shrugging, he reached into his pocket again. And as before, while I was not looking, he placed another coin into the plate. Still, I stood there, holding the plate.

When I looked at the boy again, he was frowning. Turning both of his pockets inside out, he said, "That's enough, Pastor. That's all I got."

"That's enough, Pastor." This may be the general sentiment when pastors sermonize on money. Yet, materialism is all around us: TV, radio, internet, magazine covers and Madison Avenue commercials, direct mail and infomercials. "Act now, and for only ninety-nine cents more. . . ." You know the rest.

The constant message is HAVING IS LIVING and MONEY IS HAPPINESS. And on our own, none of us are immune to this message. In Scripture, God neither commends nor condemns wealth. But He repeatedly warns us of its limitations and dangers.

## Money Can't Save

He was a man who had everything. Youth. Great wealth. Power. All the attributes the world craves. Yet, something was missing from this rich young ruler's life—something that his vast wealth could not obtain; namely, the certainty of eternal life, and with it, peace of heart and mind.

And so the rich young man asked Jesus, "Good Teacher, what shall I do that I may inherit eternal life?" Mark 10:17. This was not a casual question, nor was it a trick question like those often posed by the religious leaders of Israel. The rich man ran to Jesus. And when he asked his question, he did so on bended knees.

Startling, isn't it? This young man had everything, but was still unhappy and uncertain about his salvation. How many people are like him? How many have money in the bank, but only emptiness in their hearts?

Used wisely, money can accomplish wonderful things, but it can't save anyone from sin or purchase eternal life. Regardless of the size of the bank account, the spaciousness of the home, the make of the automobile, or the number of carats in the diamond; if we don't have Jesus Christ by faith, we have nothing of eternal value.

## Works Can't Save

"What shall I do?" asked the rich man. His assumption was that he *could* do something to inherit eternal life. This is always the assumption of human nature and always the teaching of manmade religions.

Yet, human works can never purchase salvation or bring peace of mind. Paul wrote to the Ephesians, "For by grace you have been saved through faith, and that not of yourselves; it is the gift of God, not of works, lest anyone should boast," Ephesians 2:8-9.

You and I know this lesson very well. But the rich young ruler didn't know it at all. This is why Jesus directed him to the law of God, saying, "You know the commandments,"

Mark 10:19. A serious appraisal of his life should have led the rich man to conclude that he could not keep God's commandments perfectly.

Only, how did the rich man answer Jesus? "Teacher, all these things I have kept from my youth," Mark 10:20. Desiring to turn the man away from self-trust to trusting in God, Jesus lovingly gave him a commandment he was not able to keep. "One thing you lack: Go your way, sell whatever you have and give to the poor, and you will have treasure in heaven; and come, take up the cross, and follow Me," Mark 10:21. Rather than part with his wealth, the rich man turned away from Christ.

## Only God Can Save

Jesus neither commended nor condemned wealth. But He, too, warned against its limitations and dangers. "Children," He told His disciples, "how hard it is for those who trust in riches to enter the kingdom of God! It is easier for a camel to go through the eye of a needle than for a rich man to enter the kingdom of God," Mark 10:24-25.

At this, the disciples were greatly astonished. Why? Because if the rich can't earn their way to heaven, who can? If money can't buy forgiveness, what can? If human works can't obtain eternal life, what can? Thankfully, God can and God has through the suffering, death, and resurrection of His Son, Jesus Christ.

As Jesus said, "With men it is impossible, but not with God; for with God all things are possible," Mark 10:27.

# First Miracle, Lasting Impressions

John 2:1-11

*As the saying goes, "First impressions are lasting impressions." So, what lasting impressions should we have from Christ's first miracle?*

All of us go through difficulties. And when we do, we're often tempted to doubt God's goodness, wisdom, love, and power. We find ourselves asking questions we hate to ask: "Where is God?" "Why isn't He helping?" "Does He even care?" Yet, the God revealed to us in Scripture loves us beyond measure, and is intimately involved in every aspect of our lives. This is evident from Christ's first miracle in Cana of Galilee.

**God Is Involved**

Changing water into wine was a miracle. But the circumstances in which Jesus chose to perform this miracle were no less miraculous.

The location of this miracle was not Jerusalem or the temple mount or the luxurious palace of King Herod; rather, it was the small, don't-blink-or-you'll-miss-it town of Cana in Galilee. The reason for this miracle was not a national crisis or natural disaster, but a shortage of wine. The recipients of this miracle were not kings or generals or celebrities; instead, they were two newlyweds whose names we don't even know.

What does this teach us about our God; that He is distant and disinterested, or that He is involved in every detail and problem of our lives—including a matter as minor as a shortage of wine? And if the miracle at Cana is not enough to convince us of God's involvement, then let us contemplate the cross, where Jesus sacrificed Himself for our sins. That is involvement.

## God Acts in His Time and Way

Commentators often focus on the mild rebuke Jesus gave to Mary: "Woman, what does your concern have to do with Me? My hour has not yet come," John 2:4. Yet, I believe that this mild rebuke was also an invitation. By it Jesus was saying, "You've brought this problem, this shortage of wine, to My attention. Now trust Me to act at the right time and in the right way. You know Who I am."

Mary understood this, and therefore told the servants, "Whatever He says to you, do it," John 2:5. In other words, *Mary expected Jesus to do a miracle.* Shouldn't we? He may not act in our hour or way, but He will act in His hour and way.

## God's Solution Is Always Extraordinary

When you and I are willing to wait for God to act, the outcome will always be infinitely greater than anything we could have imagined or accomplished on our own. Said differently, God will change ordinary water into extraordinary wine.

Abraham had no idea where God was leading him, but at the end of his journey he found himself in the Promised Land. Job went through heartache and great loss. Yet, Scripture describes the end of his life this way: "Now the LORD blessed the latter days of Job more than his beginning," Job 42:12.

Why does this always surprise us? How can we go through life expecting the worst from God when, in Jesus Christ, He has already given us the best He has to give?

Don't leave the wedding of Cana thinking only "what a beautiful bride," or "what a handsome groom" or "what extraordinary wine." Leave Cana knowing that God will reveal His majesty in even the minor matters of your life, too.

# God Is Faithful

1 Corinthians 1:3-9

*Everything about the Christian life depends on God's faithfulness. So, is God faithful to us or not?*

The month of January was named for the Roman god *Janus*; the god of doors, gates, bridges, and by extension, the passageway between the Old Year and the New. In Roman mythology Janus was depicted with two faces: one face looking backward, the other face looking forward.

The month of January has the same two faces. In January we look back on the Old Year and forward to the New. We review and anticipate, analyze and predict. We compose endless lists like "The Ten Best Movies" and "The Ten Worst Investments."

However, two faces looking in opposite directions can also suggest indecision or uncertainty. We may wonder, "What will happen to me in the New Year? Will I stay healthy or grow sick? Will I succeed or fail, gain or lose? Will my marriage improve? Will my job last? Will my car need an expensive repair?"

Amid such uncertainty, a phrase like "have a happy New Year" has a hollow ring. Thankfully, there is an infinitely better phrase with which to welcome the New Year—in fact, three of the most important words you will ever know: "God is faithful," 1 Corinthians 1:9. In Greek, the phrase is more literally "faithful is God." Faithful is the first word in the sentence, and therefore the word emphasized.

## God's Faithfulness in Scripture

When faced with hardships and heartaches, we may question the faithfulness of God. Yet, this is precisely why Scripture contains so many declarations of God's faithfulness.

"Forever, O LORD, Your word is settled in heaven. Your *faithfulness* endures to all generations," Psalm 119:89-90. "He who calls you is *faithful*, who also will do it," 1 Thessalonians 5:24. "Therefore let those who suffer according to the will of God commit their souls to Him in doing good, as to a *faithful* Creator," 1 Peter 4:19. Or simply, "God is *faithful*," 1 Corinthians 1:9.

We are emotional beings. When we experience heartbreak or difficulties, our emotions may distort our view of God. This is why we must stay close to the Scriptures. For in the Scriptures God's own testimony about His faithfulness is loud and clear. He is faithful to us, always faithful, *semper fi*, even when we feel He is not. We have His Word on it.

**Faithfulness Is in God's Nature**

Paul wrote in 2 Timothy 2:13, "If we are faithless, He remains faithful; He cannot deny Himself." In other words, faithfulness is not only something God does; faithfulness is something God is. Faithfulness is part of God's divine nature.

Consider what this means for your hope, home, and happiness. Because God is faithful, His faithfulness depends entirely on Him, not on you. Because God is faithful, His thoughts and actions toward you are guided by that faithfulness. Because God is faithful, even the difficulties He allows in your life are the result of His faithfulness. Because God is faithful, He will never stop loving you, protecting and providing for you, or forgiving you when you turn to Him in repentance and faith.

Because God is faithful, His every promise to you will be fulfilled: deliverance amid trouble, salvation, the forgiveness of sins in Jesus Christ; everything from daily bread to eternal life. As Paul wrote in 1 Corinthians 1:8-9, He "will also confirm you to the end, that you may be blameless in the day of our Lord Jesus Christ. God is faithful, by whom you were called into the fellowship of His Son, Jesus Christ our Lord."

**Only God Can Be So Faithful**

God's other attributes also guarantee His faithfulness. God is omniscient, meaning He knows everything. And because He knows everything about you, He will faithfully give you what you need, not necessarily what you want. "For your Father knows the things you have need of before you ask Him," Matthew 6:8. You may not need to win the Publishers Clearing House Sweepstakes. However, you may need a difficulty in your life to strengthen your faith and bring you closer to God.

God is omnipotent, that is, all-powerful. And as such, He will faithfully force even the worst circumstances to serve your best interests.

God is also omnipresent, meaning present everywhere. He will faithfully be with you in every condition, situation, and location; whether at home or the office, whether in church or the operating room.

And because God is immutable, that is, unchanging, His faithfulness toward you will never change either. As the author of Hebrews noted, "Jesus Christ is the same yesterday, today, and forever," Hebrews 13:8. The same in love. The same in compassion. The same in forgiveness. The same in faithfulness.

Whether you are healthy or sick, rich or poor, young or old, male or female, a dignitary or a nobody; if you want to know how faithful God is, look at the cross of Jesus Christ. Read the glorious words in verses 38 and 39 of Romans 8: "For I am persuaded that neither death nor life, nor angels nor principalities nor powers, nor things present nor things to come, nor height nor depth, nor any other created thing, shall be able to separate us from the love of God which is in Christ Jesus our Lord."

Why? Because God is faithful.

# God's Kind of Love

1 Corinthians 13

*To approach this majestic chapter of First Corinthians is to recognize, as Moses did at the burning shrub, that we are standing on holy ground, in the very presence of God's kind of love.*

Many associate 1 Corinthians 13 with weddings. This is understandable. The chapter speaks of the same committed love required in marriage. In fact, when Paul urged Christian husbands to "love your wives, just as Christ loved the church and gave Himself for her," Ephesians 5:25, he used the same Greek word for love found throughout 1 Corinthians 13.

However, when Paul wrote 1 Corinthians 13, he was not addressing blushing brides or handsome grooms; rather, he was speaking to a Christian congregation sorely lacking in Christian love. The Christians in Corinth were arguing over favorite pastors, abusing Christian liberty and the Lord's Supper, tolerating immorality, suing each other in court, and envying spiritual gifts. This was the setting in which Paul wrote his great chapter on love—not just any kind of love, but God's kind of love.

**Agape Love**

Ancient Greek had several words for love, each with a distinct meaning. *PHILOS* meant the love between good friends. *EROS* meant sensual love, as in the word erotic. *STORGE* meant kind affection. And *AGAPE*, the supreme form of love, meant a relentlessly committed, self-sacrificing love that insisted on loving despite the cost of its love or the unworthiness of its object.

Classical Greek writers never used the word *AGAPE* to

describe love. They could not conceive of such love existing in any human being or even in any of their Olympian gods. It remained for the New Testament writers, guided by inspiration of the Holy Spirit, to give the word *AGAPE* its richest, fullest definition. They used *AGAPE* to describe the kind of love that God lavished upon the world in Jesus Christ; the kind of love, therefore, that Christians were to show others. The apostle John wrote of Jesus, "By this we know love, because He laid down His life for us. And we also ought to lay down our lives for the brethren," 1 John 3:16.

## The Priority of Love

God's kind of love must be a priority in our lives and ministries. Without it, as Paul explained in 1 Corinthians 13:1-3, we have nothing, we gain nothing, and we are nothing. Without God's kind of love—that self-sacrificing, truth-telling, evil-shunning love—orthodoxy is meaningless, gospel outreach is meaningless, the largest buildings, budgets, and Sunday attendances are meaningless.

Many churches today are willing to talk about love. But they are not willing to talk about God's kind of love, which of necessity means talking about sin, grace, faith, and the cross of Jesus Christ.

## The Practice of Love

God's kind of love is not simply talk; it's action. Throughout 1 Corinthians 13:4-7, love is the doer of the action. It acts for its own sake. It doesn't wait for a change in its object, but instead acts to change its object.

So we, too, as grateful recipients of God's love, decide to act according to His will, whether we feel like acting or not. We decide to be patient, because God is patient. We decide to be kind, because God is kind. We decide to forgive, because God forgives. We decide to go on loving, because God goes on loving. "My little children," wrote John, "let us not love in word or in tongue, but in deed and in truth," 1 John 3:18.

## The Permanence of Love

"And now abide faith, hope, love, these three; but the greatest of these is love," 1 Corinthians 13:13. This is a remarkable statement, isn't it? Love is greater than faith. Love is greater than hope. How can this be?

Faith and hope have to do with this life, when, to use Paul's description, "we see in a mirror, dimly," 1 Corinthians 13:12. But one day soon, when the Lord Jesus returns, faith will become sight, and hope will become reality. Everything that so many have counted so dear in this life—fame, fortune, power, education, homes, wardrobes—will pass away. And what will remain is God's kind of love: His love for us and our love for Him.

Then, for all eternity, you and I will fully know God's kind of love, as that same love from eternity has fully known us.

# Identity Crisis

## John 13:31-35

*What do people think when they observe our language and behavior, our choices and priorities? Do they immediately identify us as Christ's disciples?*

What do those outside of the Christian Church think when they peer inside; when they see our behavior, priorities, responses to hardship, and especially our treatment of fellow Christians? Can they tell we are Christians? Can they easily recognize us as disciples of Jesus?

In John 13:31-35, Jesus addressed this important matter of Christian identity, and in doing so, He described the one characteristic more than any other that would clearly identify us as His disciples. What is it? Love. Not just any kind of love, but Christ's kind of love. He said, "A new commandment I give to you, that you love one another; as I have loved you, that you also love one another. By this all will know that you are My disciples, if you have love for one another." What kind of love is Christ's love?

### A Love of Selfless Service

During Christ's earthly ministry, His disciples saw many demonstrations of His love. Yet, during the Last Supper, only hours before His crucifixion, Jesus demonstrated His love in a way the disciples could never have imagined.

Standing, Jesus removed His outer garment, wrapped a towel about His waist, knelt, and began to wash the disciples' feet. Did a servant do this? No. Did one of the disciples do this? No. Would you or I have done this? No. Yet, God did. The same God who created the universe dropped to His hands and knees to wash filthy feet. His was a selfless love. And when you and I serve others selflessly, we are reflecting Christ's love and showing ourselves to be His disciples.

### A Completely Undeserved Love

Did even one disciple deserve to have his filthy feet washed by God? Has any person on earth ever deserved to be washed clean and forgiven in the priceless blood of Christ? Yet, despite our unworthiness, Jesus died for our sins. Indeed, it is in God's love for the undeserving that we glimpse the extent of His great love.

Paul wrote in Romans 5:8, "But God demonstrates His own love toward us, in that while we were still sinners, Christ died for us." When you and I love the undeserving, we are reflecting Christ's love and showing ourselves to be His disciples.

### A Determined Love

We read of Jesus in John 13:1, "Having loved His own who were in the world, He loved them to the end." Jesus loved His disciples to the end of His life, knowing full well the agonies which lay ahead in the ridiculing, scourging, and crucifixion.

Jesus also loved His disciples to the end of their lives, in spite of their sinfulness, weakness, forgetfulness, and faithlessness. And He has loved us in exactly the same way. When you and I love others "to the end," we are reflecting Christ's love and showing ourselves to be His disciples.

### An Active Love

At a time when Israel's religious leaders often refused to help the helpless, Jesus went to all the towns and villages, teaching, healing, forgiving, lifting the weights that only God could carry, and calling all to repentance and faith. His was an endlessly active love. A love which at the Last Supper stood up, stooped down, rolled up its sleeves, and washed filthy feet.

Christians talk often about love, and rightly so. But talk isn't enough, is it? According to John 3:16, "God so loved the world that He. . ." What? Sat quietly? Rang for room service? Went on vacation? No. Because God so loved, He acted. He gave His only begotten Son.

As Christians, our love must be active, too. When you and I put our love into action, we are reflecting Christ's love and showing ourselves to be His disciples.

## A Truthful Love

Can you name even one instance when Jesus changed or twisted His teaching to make it more palatable? Of course not. Jesus never told His listeners what they wanted to hear, but rather what they needed to hear: namely, the truth. The truth of God's Word. The truth about sin and punishment, grace and salvation, faith and forgiveness. He prayed, "Sanctify them by Your truth. Your word is truth," John 17:17.

Sadly, many churches today preach about love, but not a love of the truth. Yet, is it love to preach only what people want to hear? Is it love to compromise confession in order to increase attendance, revenue, or television ratings? No. This is not love. It's folly.

Paul wrote this about preaching truth: "that we should no longer be children, tossed to and fro and carried about with every wind of doctrine, by the trickery of men, in the cunning craftiness of deceitful plotting, but, speaking the truth in love, may grow up in all things into Him who is the head—Christ," Ephesians 4:14-15.

When you and I love enough to preach the truth, we are reflecting Christ's love and showing ourselves to be His disciples.

"A new commandment I give to you," He said, "that you love one another; as I have loved you, that you also love one another. By this all will know that you are My disciples, if you have love for one another."

IF.

# In God's Hands

John 10:22-30

*Scripture is filled with references to the mighty works of God's hands in our world, our lives, and our ministries.*

You've heard the phrase, "You're in good hands with Allstate." Allstate insurance company adopted this slogan in 1950 and has used it ever since. The slogan is a memorable one, suggesting strength, stability, skill, and above all, personal involvement. Hands touch, and touch is personal.

Imagine the many circumstances in which you would welcome the words "you're in good hands." Dropping children off for the first day of school. Undergoing surgery. Boarding an airplane. Making investments. Depending on a defense attorney. Following a military commander into battle. "Don't worry. You're in good hands."

Rejoice in this knowledge: There are no better hands, no stronger hands, no more comforting hands than the hands Jesus mentioned twice in John 10:28-29, saying, "My sheep hear My voice, and I know them, and they follow Me. And I give them eternal life, and they shall never perish; neither shall anyone snatch them out of *My Hand.* My Father, who has given them to Me, is greater than all; and no one is able to snatch them out of *My Father's hand.*"

## God Laid His Hands on You

The apostle Paul wrote in Ephesians 1:3-4, "Blessed be the God and Father of our Lord Jesus Christ, who has blessed us with every spiritual blessing in the heavenly places in Christ, just as He chose us in Him before the foundation of the world, that we should be holy and without blame before Him in love."

Contemplate this great truth: In eternity God reached out and laid His hands on you, that is, laid claim to you as His very own, and then brought you to faith through the Gospel. God did not choose you because He foresaw that you would believe. You believe because God chose you. As Paul wrote in Philippians 3:12, "Not that I have already attained, or am already perfected; but I press on, that I may lay hold of that for which Christ Jesus has already laid hold of me."

Your belief in Jesus is the proof that God laid His hands on you, that God chose you. And in a selfish, egotistical world in which we so often go unwanted, unnoticed, and unappreciated, what joy and peace you should find in this reality: You are in God's hands, because God laid His hands on you.

## God's Hands Are Leading You

When I worked at Jean O' Dell Learning Center, a school for severely disabled children, one of my responsibilities was to escort students one by one to their assigned buses. I often took them by the hand to ensure they wouldn't fall, get lost, stray into traffic, or board the wrong bus. One young woman always kissed my hands when we reached her bus. That was her way of saying, "Thanks. I trust you."

Jesus said, "My sheep hear My voice, and I know them, and they follow Me," John 10:27. His words describe a deep, abiding relationship and trust, a divine leading and confident following, a walking hand-in-hand with the Savior as He leads us—in the poetic words of Psalm 23—from birth to death, through peaks and valleys, until we "dwell in the house of the LORD forever."

And Jesus leads you as the One Who knows you. In fact, the Greek verb used for "I know them" in John 10:27 means a complete knowledge grounded in personal experience. Surely, in moments of anger, frustration, or despair, many of us have cried out, "Isn't there anyone who knows the real me? Isn't there anyone who understands me? Isn't there anyone who can see what's on the inside, not just the outside?" Yes, there is such a One. And His name is Jesus Christ. Whatever problems you may be facing, trust Jesus. Listen to His Word in the certain knowledge that He is leading you by the hand, and that He will never let you go.

## You Are Eternally Safe in God's Hands

When I was a boy, I played a game with my dad in which he would clench his fist tightly, and I would try to open it. I would use one hand, two hands; then try to wriggle my fingers into his fist, targeting his thumb or little finger—all while grunting, giggling, and using my legs for leverage. Nothing worked. His hands were too strong.

How strong are the hands of God? Is there anything more comforting than knowing that you are in the almighty hands of God, and that nothing can snatch you out of God's hands?

Nothing can come between you and God, or interfere with His love and purposes for your life. Paul wrote in Romans 8: "Yet in all these things we are more than conquerors through Him who loved us. For I am persuaded that neither death nor life, nor angels nor principalities nor powers, nor things present nor things to come, nor height nor depth, nor any other created thing, shall be able to separate us from the love of God which is in Christ Jesus our Lord."

Remember this: The hands of Christ; the hands that saved you, claimed you, lead you, protect and provide for you, will forever bear the marks of the cross. In His hands you are eternally safe.

# In Defense of Marriage and Morality

Exodus 20:14

*In our modern age, immorality is not only flaunted, it is marketed as natural, wholesome, and beneficial.*

Ted Turner, the media mogul, reportedly said, "We are living with outdated rules. The rules we are living under are the Ten Commandments. I bet no one even pays attention to them because they're too old."

Turner's view typifies that of the world, a world which either denies the existence of God or paints Him as a doting, senile Grandfather, who cares nothing about the behavior of His children so long as they "stop by the house" on Sunday mornings. Rejecting God and His law, the world lives by its own set of rules—or lack of them, calling wrong right and right wrong.

Nowhere is this disregard of God more evident than in the worldly view of marriage, adultery, and immorality. In our modern age, immorality is not only prevalent, it is marketed as natural, wholesome, and beneficial. Those who oppose the "modern" view are labeled as unloving and un-American.

To such a world, God's "You shall not commit adultery" is, as Ted Turner insisted, old and outdated. Yet, this command from God has never been more needed or more relevant.

## The Meaning of the Commandment

The Hebrew word translated as "adultery" in Exodus 20:14, *NAAPH*, literally means "to stain with a dye," and by extension, "to defile." Adultery, then, is a staining or defiling of our bodies (which are meant to be temples of the Holy Spirit) and of God's holy estate of matrimony. And as with all of God's commandments, His "You shall not commit adultery" embraces both deed and thought.

Why is this important? Human nature asserts that "it's okay to look as long as I don't touch." By contrast, Jesus said in His Sermon on the Mount, "But I say to you that whoever looks at a woman to lust for her has already committed adultery with her in his heart," Matthew 5:28. If looking leads to lusting, it is a sin and by no means acceptable to God.

Martin Luther wrote in his Large Catechism, "Therefore, this commandment is directed against all kinds of unchastity, whatever it may be called. Not only is the outward act of adultery forbidden, but also every kind of cause, motive, and means of adultery."

### The Consequences of Disobeying the Commandment

The world views adultery as natural and inevitable. The founder of Ashley Madison, the company whose advertising slogan is "life is short, have an affair" said, "People stray, that's all there is to it." According to Scripture, however, adultery is both sinful and destructive.

Adultery is not only a sin against God; it is also a sin against others, especially one's spouse and family. The long-term cost of a moment of pleasure is virtually incalculable when measured in terms of broken hearts, broken homes, and broken families. And by destroying families, adultery also undermines the God-ordained building-blocks of human society. So, is adultery as harmless as society insists?

Solomon wrote in Proverbs 6:32, "Whoever commits adultery with a woman lacks understanding; He who does so destroys his own soul." Or translated another way, "destroys his own life." His life, and the lives of many others.

### The Intent of the Commandment

God created us as sexual beings, intending the gift of sex

to be pleasurable, procreative, and reserved for the lifelong commitment of marriage. He also intended marriage to be the loving, stable framework in which to raise children. Sadly, there is nothing loving, stable, or committed about adultery. It is a selfish, destructive act. This is why God prohibited it.

No one likes to be told "no," especially the Old Sinful Nature. Yet, even at a purely human level, saying "no" is paramount to safety. Loving parents tell their children "no" to protect them, not to deprive them. And if this is true of earthly parents, how much truer is it of our perfect Father in heaven? God did not say "you shall not commit adultery" to deprive us, but to prevent us from hurting ourselves, our spouses, our families, and ultimately, society itself.

### Our Response to the Commandment

As Christians, our sincere desire is to please the Lord. Yet, despite our best efforts, we still sin against the Sixth Commandment—if not in deed, then in thought. With Paul we lament in Romans 7, "For I know that in me (that is, in my flesh) nothing good dwells; for to will is present with me, but how to perform what is good I do not find. . . . O wretched man that I am! Who will deliver me from this body of death?" Oh, praise God for the answer: "I thank God—through Jesus Christ our Lord!"

In Christ we find the forgiveness of our sins. In Christ we find the will and strength to walk the way of God's commandments. And when we are tempted to commit adultery, in Christ we find the ability to say with Joseph in Genesis 39:9, "How then can I do this great wickedness, and sin against God?"

The Sixth Commandment forbids adultery, But the immeasurable cost of Christ's sacrifice, even more than the commandment, shows how wrong, how out of godly character, and how ungrateful the act of adultery really is.

# Invested

Luke 19:11-27

*God is fully invested in us. How invested are we in the work of His kingdom?*

In the *Parable of the Minas*, a nobleman travels to a distant country to receive a kingship. Before leaving, he provides each of his servants with a single mina—worth about three months' wages—then instructs them to "put the minas to work" in his kingdom.

Of course, the nobleman in the parable is Jesus. We are the servants. So the question is, what are we doing with *our* minas—our gifts, abilities, resources—as we eagerly await the return of the King? Are we investing ourselves in the work of God's kingdom? Are we like the servants whose minas produced more minas? Or are we like the one servant who hid his mina in a cloth, more concerned with losing it than using it?

## God Is Invested in You

When studying the *Parable of the Minas*, many focus first on what each servant did with his mina. Did he invest it? Did he waste it? These are important questions. Only the primary lesson of this parable—investing oneself in the work of God's kingdom—does not begin with the minas. It begins with the servants and their relationship to the nobleman. For without that relationship, the servants would have no minas to invest, no king to serve, and no reward to expect.

Our investment in the work of God's kingdom begins with an understanding of how invested God is in each of us. He created us. He saved us. He privileged us to be His servants. And most of all, He gave His one and only Son to save us from our sins. Talk about an investment.

Peter wrote of God's investment, saying, "You were not redeemed with corruptible things, like silver or gold, from your aimless conduct received by tradition from your fathers, but with the precious blood of Christ, as of a lamb without blemish and without spot," 1 Peter 1:18-19.

Christians often wonder, "How can I be more involved in the work of God's kingdom? Where can I find the courage to invite a friend to church or to participate in an outreach activity?" The answer is NOT to first read a book on evangelism or take a course on witnessing, as helpful as these resources may be.

Resources like these explain the mechanics, but they cannot impart the power. As Paul wrote to the Romans, the power to serve Christ and bear witness to Christ comes from the Gospel itself. "For I am not ashamed of the gospel of Christ," he said, "for it is the power of God to salvation for everyone who believes," Romans 1:16.

Ask yourself, "What has Jesus done for me?" For therein lies the power and willingness to invest yourself in the nobleman's business and in the work of God's kingdom.

## God Has Given You a Mina

In the *Parable of the Minas*, the nobleman calls ten of his servants and gives *each of them* one mina. My heart breaks when I hear Christians say things like "I'm not important to this congregation." "I don't have anything to share." "I'm too old." "I'm of no value." I have no part in this gospel ministry."

Nothing could be farther from the truth. God has given *you* a mina to invest in the work of His kingdom. Perhaps your mina is playing the organ for worship services; or bringing refreshments to fellowship meals; or serving as a voter, council member, usher, greeter, or lector; or the ability to support a congregation financially.

But you do have a mina from God. And your mina is as important to God and the work of His kingdom as any other Christian gift. This is why Jesus described each servant in the parable as receiving a mina—a generous amount in antiquity and even by today's standards. In God's kingdom, each mina invested is of equal value.

## God Will Bless Your Investment

When we invest ourselves in the work of God's kingdom, God will surely bless the investment. After all, our minas came from Him, and our minas belong to Him. As the hymnist wrote, "We give Thee but Thine own, whate'er the gift may be; all that we have is Thine alone, a trust, O Lord, from Thee."

In the *Parable of the Minas*, the nobleman not only called his servants, he also equipped them. He gave each servant a mina. The same is true of us. God never calls us to undertake a task in His kingdom without equipping us to do it. Someone put it this way, "God does not call the qualified. God qualifies the called."

Don't be ashamed of small accomplishments. Don't be ashamed of the size of your congregation or budget. Do you think God is ashamed of such things? In this parable, the nobleman-turned-king was as delighted with an increase of five minas as he was with ten.

For us, the issue is not the return on investment. The issue is *making* the investment. God is fully invested in us. May we be invested in Him.

# Is Anything Too Hard
# for the Lord

Genesis 18:1-14

*Only God has the power and the willingness to do
what He promises.*

Outside the tent, the men were talking. Inside the tent, near
the entrance, Sarah was carefully listening. When she heard
one of the visitors tell Abraham, "I will certainly return to you
according to the time of life, and behold, Sarah your wife shall
have a son," Genesis 18:10, Sarah laughed to herself. A silent
laugh. Yet, God heard her laughter and rebuked her. "Why did
Sarah laugh?" God asked Abraham, adding, "Is anything too
hard for the LORD?" Genesis 18:13-14.

God asks us this same question; not only when times are
good, but also amid times of pain, suffering, failure, and loss.
"Is anything too hard for the LORD?"

## No Promise Is Too Hard for the Lord to Fulfill

Political candidates make many promises: "I will do this."
"I will fix that." "I will increase prosperity and reduce taxes."
Wonderful ideas. Yet, the average American laughs at such
promises—Sarah's laugh of skepticism—because the average
politician has neither the power nor the inclination to keep his
word. By contrast, Almighty God has both the power and the
willingness to do what He promises. And where is this better
demonstrated than in the lives of Abraham and Sarah?

By the time the visitors arrived at the great trees of Mamre,
Abraham and Sarah had been waiting for their promised son
for twenty-five years. Sarah was now ninety years old.
Abraham was one hundred. Both were decades beyond the age
of childbearing. Even had they not been, Sarah was barren and

unable to have children.

No wonder Sarah laughed a skeptical laugh. No wonder she said, "After I have grown old, shall I have pleasure, my lord being old also?" Genesis 18:12. Sarah was worn out physically, emotionally, reproductively, and no doubt by the years of waiting for God to fulfill His promise.

Yet, through all the waiting, God was teaching both Abraham and Sarah a powerful lesson: "Nothing is too hard for the LORD." God kept His promise, as we're told in Genesis 21:1, "And the LORD visited Sarah as He had said, and the LORD did for Sarah as He had spoken."

God has made many promises to us, too. He has promised to love us eternally, to provide for us continually, to bless any endeavor undertaken in His name, to bring us safely from grace to glory, and to forgive our sins for the sake and sacrifice of Jesus Christ. And He will keep each promise.

And if the history of Abraham and Sarah does not convince us of this, remember, God also promised to send a Savior, and He did. The fulfillment of this greatest of promises, the coming of Christ, is the GUARANTEE that God will keep all His other promises, too. As Paul explained in 2 Corinthians 1:20, "For all the promises of God in Him are Yes, and in Him Amen, to the glory of God through us."

## No Problem Is Too Hard for the Lord to Solve

Sarah was elderly and barren. Was this problem too hard for the Lord? No. As promised, she became pregnant, and nine months later she was nursing Isaac and changing diapers. The Israelites were stranded on the shore of the Red Sea, pursued by Pharaoh's army. Was this problem too hard for the Lord? No. God parted the sea, and the Israelites passed through on dry ground. Later, the Israelites complained of no food and no water in the wilderness. Was this problem too hard for the Lord? No. God rained manna from heaven and provided water from a rock. And when the world was lost and condemned through the fall into sin, was even this problem too hard for the Lord? No. God sent His Son to be our Savior. God saved us by punishing Christ.

God has said, "Call upon Me in the day of trouble; I will deliver you, and you shall glorify Me," Psalm 50:15. Is this true or not? Is God all-powerful or not? If we think *any* problem in life is too hard for God to solve, we don't know Him as well as we should.

## No Person Is Too Hard for the Lord to Save

Paul wrote to Timothy, "And I thank Christ Jesus our Lord who has enabled me, because He counted me faithful, putting me into the ministry, although I was formerly a blasphemer, a persecutor, and an insolent man; but I obtained mercy because I did it ignorantly in unbelief. And the grace of our Lord was exceedingly abundant, with faith and love which are in Christ Jesus. This is a faithful saying and worthy of all acceptance, that Christ Jesus came into the world to save sinners, of whom I am chief," 1 Timothy 1:12-15.

These words convey a deep sense of unworthiness—the same unworthiness we feel when we evaluate our lives, sins, and weaknesses. Yet, no matter who we are; no matter what we've done; no matter how stubborn, sinful, and rebellious we've been; the precious blood of Christ cleanses us and saves us when, by God's pure grace, we trust in Jesus as our Savior.

As the hymnist wrote: "Today Thy mercy calls us to wash away our sin. However great our trespass, whatever we have been, however long from mercy our hearts have turned away, Thy precious blood can cleanse us and make us white today."

Is anything too hard for the Lord? Anything at all? Ask Abraham and Sarah. Ask Saul the persecutor, who became Paul the apostle. Ask Jesus Himself, Who told His disciples, "With men this is impossible, but with God all things are possible."

# Learning from Tragedy

## Luke 13:1-9

*There is no happy way to commemorate the tragedy of September 11, 2001, but we can learn from it.*

Many of us remember September 11, 2001—where we were, what we were doing, who we were with, and especially the horrific scenes we were watching on TV. The planes slamming into the Twin Towers. The explosions, flames, and black smoke billowing into a bright blue sky. The desperate people leaping to their deaths. The Twin Towers, the very symbol of American economic power, finally collapsing in an avalanche of dust, debris, concrete, and twisted steel.

What lessons were learned from 9/11? We learned that we were vulnerable to terrorism, that government agencies were not sharing vital intelligence data, and that the enemies we faced—Islamic terrorists—were willing to commit the most heinous crimes in the name of their religion.

But amid the tragedy and rubble of September 11, 2001, we also learned good things about ourselves: the courage and resilience, the selfless acts of complete strangers, and our willingness, if only briefly, to unite as "we the people of the United States of America."

There is no happy way to commemorate the worst terrorist attack on American soil. But we can learn from it, not simply how to better protect the homeland, but how to better protect the heart from the spiritual complacency that can lead to an even greater tragedy. You won't find this lesson in the official 9/11 Committee Report. You will find it in the words of Jesus in Luke 13:1-9.

Two tragedies are described in this text: the slaughter of Jewish worshipers by Pontius Pilate, and the collapse of a tower that killed eighteen people. The first tragedy was deliberate; the second was accidental. But we can learn from both.

## Asking Why

Tragedies always make us ask "why?" Why were Jewish worshipers killed in the temple? Why were eighteen bystanders killed when the Tower of Siloam collapsed? Why did terrorists fly planes into the Twin Towers? Why did nearly three thousand people die on September 11, 2001, people who did nothing more that fateful day than go to work or catch a flight?

Yet, when Jesus discussed the tragedies in Luke 13:1-9, He did not address the question of "why." Nor did He engage in a defense of God's goodness, kindness, and fairness—the divine attributes so often impugned in times of tragedy. "What kind of God would allow such a thing?" How many times was this question asked on September 11, 2001? How many times have we asked it since?

So very often, however, you and I don't know the "why" of a tragedy. In fact, in Luke 13:1-9, Jesus carefully explained that the deaths of the Jewish worshipers and eighteen innocent bystanders had nothing to do with who they were or what they had done. He wanted us to learn from the WHAT of these tragedies, and not to get lost in the WHY.

## A Sinful World

This may come as a surprise, but Almighty God is not the cause of every tragedy, disaster, problem, flat tire, and food-borne illness in the United States or throughout the world; though He is often blamed for such—and has been since Adam and Eve fell into sin. "Your fault, God." No, it wasn't God's fault. It was *their* fault. Their fault tragedies exist. Their fault things go wrong. Their fault the earth is a place of decay instead of a place of perfection. Do you know why insurance companies label natural disasters or unexplained accidents "acts of God"? Because they have no one else to blame.

Yes, tragedies happen, but consider the setting in which they happen. A world in which mudslides bury villages, and AIDS kills millions, and children die from starvation, and whole families are killed by drunk drivers, and terrorists fly planes into buildings, and desperate people numb themselves with drugs or alcohol because they "can't take it anymore." This is not the world God created for us. It is the world we created for ourselves. A world of sin, and therefore a world of tragedy.

## Limited Time

Even the world says, "Only two things are certain, death and taxes." Yet, between these two, we generally pay more attention to taxes than death. Ironically, we act as if we will live forever, when in reality we may die tomorrow. Doesn't every tragedy teach us this lesson?

Did the Jewish worshipers in Luke 13:1-9 expect to die when they left for church? Did the eighteen people crushed by the tower expect to die when they went for a stroll by the Pool of Siloam? Did the nearly three thousand who perished on September 11, 2001, expect to die when they got out of bed that morning, showered, dressed, kissed their spouse, hugged their children, and hurried off to work? No. But death came for them anyway. And one day it will come for us, too. That is the reality. So the question is, how can we face death with absolute confidence?

## An Urgent Need for Jesus Christ

If ignoring our own mortality is foolish, then ignoring our need for Christ is the worst of tragedies. This is why Jesus equated the two tragedies in Luke 13 with the need for repentance, saying, "but unless you repent you will all likewise perish," Luke 13:3,5.

The word *perish* in these verses does not mean physical death, as if Jesus were saying, "Repent, and you will live to be a hundred. Repent, and you will never be sick." No, this is the *perish* of John 3:16, the eternal death and punishment from which Jesus Christ came to save us: "For God so loved the world that He gave His only begotten Son, that whoever believes in Him should not PERISH but have everlasting life."

In a narrow sense, repentance means godly sorrow over sin and turning to God for forgiveness through Christ. But repentance means more than this. The Greek word for repent literally means "a change of mind." Hence, a change of direction. A change of life and lifestyle. A change of everything for the simple reason that today, while we are living, is our time of grace; and Jesus Christ is the only way to be saved. And if these two things are true—that TODAY is our time of grace, and that JESUS CHRIST is the only way to be saved—should our salvation be a priority or an afterthought?

God's grace is limitless. But our time to receive it is not. Consequently, the Bible never speaks of salvation in terms of tomorrow, but always in terms of today. "Today, if you will hear His voice, do not harden your hearts," Hebrews 3:7-8. "Behold, now is the accepted time; behold, now is the day of salvation," 2 Corinthians 6:2.

# Ministers of Christ

1 Corinthians 2:1-5

*The goal of preaching is not to have parishioners say, "My, what a beautiful sermon"; but rather, "My, what a beautiful Savior!"*

The phrase "ministers of Christ" is broader than the office of the public ministry. It also embraces the priesthood of all believers in Christ; that is, their God-given right and responsibility to share the gospel in whatever circumstances the Lord has placed them. Yet, we often approach our public and personal ministries with a sense of weakness, fear, and trembling. What's the solution?

**The Means Is Scripture**

Paul told the Corinthians, "And I, brethren, when I came to you, did not come with excellence of speech or of wisdom declaring to you the testimony of God," 1 Corinthians 2:1.

Corinth was in Greece, and Greece was famous for its philosophy and oratory. As early as the Fifth Century B.C., traveling teachers known as Sophists taught a discipline they called rhetoric—from the Greek word *RHEMA*, meaning words. The goal of this early rhetoric was to persuade and even manipulate listeners through powerful speeches, extensive vocabularies, flowery metaphors, and practiced gestures, often at the expense of the truth.

When Paul said that he did not "come with excellence of speech or of wisdom," he meant, "I did not come to trick, but to teach. I did not come to conceal the truth, but to reveal the truth. I did not come to impress you with my words, but to share God's words" or as he put it, "the testimony of God."

Does this mean that pastors should not strive for

excellence in preaching? No. Every sermon should be as good as it can be—good, not for the sake of being good, but good for the sake of glorifying God. Styles, vocabularies, compelling introductions and powerful conclusions are only useful if they serve the word of God and do not supplant the word of God. The goal is not to have parishioners leave church, saying, "My, what a beautiful sermon"; but rather, "My, what a beautiful Savior."

The means to ministry lies in proclaiming the Scriptures in their fullness: sin and grace, law and gospel—not in entertaining, and not in diluting the teachings of the Bible to make them more palatable or reasonable. Scripture must be the means of ministry, because Scripture is the only means through which the Spirit of God has chosen to work.

### The Message Is Christ

Paul wrote, "For I determined not to know anything among you except Jesus Christ and Him crucified," 1 Corinthians 2:2. What did Paul mean—that his teaching and preaching in Corinth consisted only of reciting the words "Jesus Christ and Him crucified"? No. He meant that "Jesus Christ and Him crucified" was always the focus of his message.

Early in my ministry, someone advised me to look for Christ on every page of the Bible. I wish I could recall the source, because that godly advice helped shape my entire ministry. Jesus must be the focus in ministry, because Jesus is the focus of the entire Bible. And "Jesus Christ and Him crucified" must be the message, because there is no other Savior and no other way to be saved. As Jesus Himself explained, "I am the way, the truth, and the life. No one comes to the Father except through Me," John 14:6.

### The Power Is God's

Paul stated in 1 Corinthians 2:4-5, "And my speech and my preaching were not with persuasive words of human wisdom, but in demonstration of the Spirit and of power, that your faith should not be in the wisdom of men but in the power of God."

If I could change anything about my ministry, it would be the foolish assumption that I've had so often, amid so many difficult circumstances, that the power to create faith, the power to effect change, the power to return a wayward member to church, the power to enrich a troubled marriage, the power to encourage fellow Christians—that this power resided in me. It has never resided in me and never will. The power is God's. And when we finally realize this truth and put it into practice, we will not only save ourselves heartache, but carry out our public and private ministries with confidence.

Paul said, "For I am not ashamed of the gospel of Christ, for it is the power of God to salvation for everyone who believes," Romans 1:16. Do we understand what this means?

Look at your Bible. The cover may be worn. The pages may be dog-eared from use. The verses may be underlined. But there is no difference between the powerful words of Scripture and the words of power with which Jesus Christ calmed storms, healed the sick, and raised the dead.

And this is the Word He has entrusted to us.

# One for All, All for One

1 Corinthians 12:12-21, 26-27

*"One for all, and all for one." Long before the Three Musketeers said it, Paul wrote about it in 1 Corinthians 12.*

When I was a boy, my best friend was David Shaffer. David and I were next-door neighbors in Winter Haven, Florida. This was the 1950s, long before cell phones and video games, computers and internet, megabytes and twitter feeds. A time when kids still played with each other instead of with electronic devices.

And play we did, as far as our imagination would carry us. On the nearby canal we were marauding pirates. In the adjacent woods we were big-game hunters in search of mythical beasts. At times, David and I were the Three Musketeers, even though there were only two of us.

I can still see us: young, blonde-headed, bare-footed, shirtless and suntanned, crossing the two long sticks that passed for swords, and shouting in unison, "One for all, and all for one." A motto we undoubtedly borrowed from the 1960 movie, *The Three Musketeers*, instead of the 1844 novel by Alexandre Dumas.

"One for all, and all for one." Even as boys we meant the words. "We are united. We are one in purpose. What happens to you matters to me." Despite all the changes to come—moving, schools, careers, marriage and families—David Shaffer remained my best friend, my fellow Musketeer, until his untimely death at the age of thirty-nine.

"One for all, and all for one." Look closely, and you'll find the same concept, same closeness, and same commitment reflected in 1 Corinthians 12; though with a far better example than the Three Musketeers. To explain the closeness of the Christian Church—"what happens to you matters to me"—the apostle Paul used the illustration of the human body. He did this in 1 Corinthians 12, but also in Ephesians 1 and 4.

And the point of this illustration is simple. The human body has many parts. Each part is important for the well-being, health, and happiness of the whole body. Therefore, the whole body has a vested interest in the circumstances of each part. Said differently, "one for all, and all for one." And what is true of the human body is equally true of the body of believers, the Christian Church.

Consider how, after the First Pentecost, the gospel of Christ unified such diverse, formerly antagonistic groups as Jews and Gentiles, masters and slaves, wealthy and poor, educated and illiterate. At a time when slaves were considered worthless, and women were often viewed as property, the gospel declared, "For you are all one in Christ Jesus," Galatians 3:28.

This oneness in Christ is what makes selfish divisions like those in the Corinthian congregation—"My pastor is better than your pastor"—so wrong. This oneness is what makes false teaching so deplorable. Along with the dangers that false teachers present to faith, they also disrupt the unity all believers have in Christ.

**One for All**

While personal differences—race, color, gender, finances, education, social status, and so on—do not matter within the Christian community, personal gifts do. God has given each of us gifts to be used for the benefit, well-being, and happiness of the entire Christian Church. "But the manifestation of the Spirit is given to each one for the profit of all," Paul wrote in 1 Corinthians 12:7.

This means that each of us, whether young or old, organist or lector, voter or pastor, greeter or contributor, has important gifts. And what makes them important is their importance to the whole body of believers. Therefore, to think your God-given talents and abilities are unimportant is a tragedy. To fail to use them is even worse.

When I was in college and still smoking cigarettes, one of my professors took me aside and said, "Mark, you really should stop smoking." Grinning, I replied, "You mean for health reasons." "Yes," he said. "But more than that, why would you want to deprive the Christian Church of one of its gifts?"

## All for One

The complement to "one for all" is "all for one." And this really needs no explanation, does it? If you and I remember that as Christians we are all members of Christ's body, the Christian Church, through faith; if we remember how important every member of that body is to the well-being, happiness, and functionality of the whole body; then *every* member of that body should be the object of our love and concern. Not just the wealthy, but also the poor. Not just the young, but also the elderly. Not just the healthy, but also the sick and weak. Not just the people in the church pews, but also those in hospital beds and nursing homes.

This is what Paul meant when he wrote in 1 Corinthians 12:24-26, "But God composed the body, having given greater honor to that part which lacks it, that there should be no schism in the body, but that the members should have the same care for one another. And if one member suffers, all the members suffer with it; or if one member is honored, all the members rejoice with it."

As we carry out our congregational ministries, let's remember that it is this kind of genuine love and concern for each other that will tell the world who we are—Christians—and to whom we belong—Jesus Christ—more effectively than any newspaper advertisement or well-placed church sign.

# Prepared for the Journey

Psalm 121

*As Christians, our entire lives are pilgrimages.*
*We're simply passing through the Temporary on our*
*way to the Eternal.*

On a clear August morning in 1968, my grandfather and I loaded his old black Studebaker, backed down the driveway, turned right on Lake Howard Drive, and set off for Immanuel Lutheran High School in Eau Claire, Wisconsin. As we left, I had no idea that I would not return to Florida permanently until 2010. The intervening forty-two years, 1968 to 2010, became a long series of homecomings and departures, each more emotional than the last.

I remember that August morning as if it were yesterday: the hugs and well wishes, the suggestion of tears in my father's eyes, the way my family stood and waved and waved until the old black Studebaker disappeared on Lake Howard Drive.

And I remember the words of my great grandmother, Sophie Fischer; who, holding my face in her arthritic hands, said, "Mark, may God go with you and keep you safe on your journey." In her mind there was no better way to send me on my journey than to entrust me to the safekeeping and vigilant care of Almighty God.

Admittedly, when young, I found this farewell unusual, overly concerned. "God go with you and keep you safe." But why? What could go wrong? I was young, happy, healthy, and invincible. Later, however, when older and more fully aware of the frailty and dangers of life, I realized the wisdom of my great grandmother's words—words which bore a remarkable resemblance to Psalm 121.

Psalm 121 has been called the Traveler's Psalm. Jewish pilgrims may have used it to prepare for the long, arduous journey to Jerusalem during religious festivals. Yet, this psalm has great meaning for us, too. As children of God, our entire lives are pilgrimages. We're simply passing through the Temporary on our way to the Eternal. What will prepare us for the rigors of the journey? Psalm 121 has the answers.

## God's Presence

All of us have taken trips. How much planning did we do? We may have spent hours online searching for the best fares, accommodations, and attractions. If driving, we may have taken the car in for a tune-up; or even washed it in the mistaken belief that a clean car is a more reliable car. Before leaving home, we did the laundry, packed suitcases, stopped the mail, boarded the pet, and asked the neighbor to watch the premises.

But where in our trip preparations did we remember God? Was He first or last, before the ticket purchase or after the baggage claim? Yes, our own travel preparations are important. But as Christians, do we truly believe that *our* preparations are ultimately what keep us safe and lead us to our destination?

Although we often place God last in our planning, Psalm 121 places Him first. In fact, God is mentioned nine times in the psalm's eight short verses. "My help comes from the LORD," wrote the psalmist. And don't hurry past the name LORD. The Hebrew is *YAVEH*, a verb meaning "I AM," the one name for God more than any other that emphasizes His eternal presence and unchanging faithfulness.

So you ask, "God, are You with me on this journey?" And true to His name He answers, "I AM." You ask, "God, are You with me in this troubled marriage?" He answers, "I AM." You ask, "Are You with me in this hospital room?" He answers, "I AM." To know that the LORD is Your helper, that the LORD is always with you, is to be prepared for the journey.

## God's Power

After stating that our helper is the LORD, the psalmist adds the words, "who made heaven and earth," Psalm 121:2. This phrase is used at least fifteen times in Scripture, along with multitudes of other references to God as the Creator. And significantly, many of these references occur within a context of human weakness and impossibility.

God made the universe from nothing. Do you think your personal problems are too hard for the LORD? Do you think your troubled relationship is too hard for the LORD? Do you think the circumstances in your congregation are too hard for the LORD? The reality is, our problems are not too big; our view of God is often too small. To know this is to be prepared for the journey.

## God's Involvement

The psalmist wrote, "He will not allow your foot to be moved," Psalm 121:3. Do these words mean that Jewish pilgrims never slipped or fell when they traveled the rough roads and rugged mountain passes to Jerusalem? No. But the words do convey the promise of divine protection, as do the references to "the LORD is your shade at your right hand," verse 5, and "the sun shall not strike you by day, nor the moon by night," verse 6. Truthfully, you and I have no idea how many times and in how many ways God protects us each day, or in the words of the psalm, "keeps our foot from being moved"—the illness we didn't get, the accident we didn't have, the fall we didn't take, the car we didn't hit.

However, the phrase "He will not allow your foot to be moved" also speaks of God's personal involvement in our daily lives. How staggering to think that the God Who created heaven and earth is so involved in our lives, problems, and undertakings that He cares about one of our feet slipping.

But then, should we expect anything less from the God Who led the Israelites through the wilderness, without letting one of their sandals wear out? Even more so, should we expect anything less from the God who came to share in our humanity and suffer and die for our sins? That is personal involvement. To know this is to be prepared for the journey.

## God's Vigilance

As parents, we wish we could watch over our children twenty-four hours a day, but we can't. We wish we lived closer, but we don't. Yet, twice we're told in Psalm 121 that Almighty God "shall neither slumber nor sleep," verses 3 and 4. In Hebrew there is a difference between the words *slumber* and *sleep*. The former has to do with indifference; the latter with exhaustion.

But God is never indifferent towards us. How do we know? He gave His one and only Son to save us from our sins. And God never wearies in helping us. How do we know? He made heaven and earth. This means that every minute of every hour of every year of your Christian journey, Almighty God is watching over you with His loving heart and wide-open eyes.

Consequently, His promise to you is this: "The Lord shall preserve your going out and your coming in from this time forth, and even forevermore," Psalm 121:8. And to know this is to be prepared for the journey.

# Prepared to Witness

1 Peter 3:8-16

*When the lordship of Jesus Christ is preeminent in your home-life, church-life, and work-life, people will ask you for the "reason for the hope that is in you."*

It was late on Christmas Eve. All the presents were beneath the tree, except for one. Before going to bed, I still had to assemble a tricycle for my youngest son, Andrew. Removing the parts from the box, I glanced at the instructions, yawned, then tore them up and threw them away. At midnight, I had no desire to read microscopic print printed in three languages. "Besides," I told myself, "I don't need instructions. How hard can it be to assemble a toddler's tricycle?"

For the next three hours I struggled with that how-hard-can-it-be tricycle. When I was done, one rear wheel wobbled. The handlebars were crooked. And most troubling of all, there were leftover parts I could not explain.

Yes, you're right. I should have read the instructions. And if that's true of a tricycle, it is certainly true of life.

There is an instruction manual for life. It's called the Bible—God's HOW-TO BOOK for how to be saved; how to live a godly life; how to forgive; how to have a happy marriage; how to raise children; how to find comfort, strength, and confidence; how to stop worrying; how to prepare for death and obtain eternal life; and even how to be a witness for Jesus Christ.

## Be Reverent

When given the opportunity to witness, we often focus on who we are and what we have. "Am I experienced or a novice?" "Do I speak eloquently or haltingly?" "Am I outgoing or shy?" "Do I have professionally-designed outreach brochures or homemade materials?" Yet, according to the apostle Peter, our first focus should not be on who we are but on who Jesus Christ is. He is the Lord. He is the omnipotent Son of God. He is the One who commissioned His church to proclaim the saving gospel, saying, "All authority has been given to Me in heaven and on earth," Matthew 28:18.

Peter wrote, "But sanctify the Lord God in your hearts," 1 Peter 3:15. In the Greek, the word *Lord* is placed first in the sentence for extreme emphasis. When preparing to witness or canvass a neighborhood, remember that Jesus is LORD; that the Lord Jesus is right there with you. And if you are part of a small, struggling Christian congregation, remember that there is always One in attendance who goes unseen and unrecorded, but should never go unrecognized: The Lord of heaven and earth.

## Be Ready

When the lordship of Christ is preeminent in your home-life, church-life, and work-life, people will ask you the "reason for the hope that is in you," 1 Peter 3:15. It is important not only to recognize these opportunities, but also to be ready to use them. Where does this readiness come from? The Word of God.

Paul wrote to Timothy, "All Scripture is given by inspiration of God, and is profitable for doctrine, for reproof, for correction, for instruction in righteousness, that the man of God may be complete, THOROUGHLY EQUIPPED for every good work," 2 Timothy 3:16-17. And this includes the good work of witnessing.

The best preparation for witnessing has always been and will always be the study of God's Word. The more you learn from Scripture, the more prepared you will be to witness. Church is preparation. Bible class is preparation. Family devotions are preparation. Each time you study God's Word, you are preparing—no, better said, you are being prepared—prepared by the Holy Spirit to bear witness to Jesus Christ. Your testimony about Christ need not be eloquent. It only needs to be heartfelt, that is, from your heart where, as Peter stated, Jesus Christ is enthroned as Lord and Savior.

## Be Respectful

Peter said, "and always be ready to give a defense to everyone who asks you a reason for the hope that is in you, with meekness and fear," 1 Peter 3:15.

With meekness. With respect. These words need no explanation, do they? How can we talk about God's forgiveness without being forgiving? How can we talk about God's patience without being patient? Our behavior will either lend credibility to our Christian witnessing or undermine it. Our deeds will either proclaim the lordship of Christ or deny it.

Which type of witness do we want to be?

# Racing for the Crown

1 Corinthians 9:24-27

*In the race of faith, the goal is not to win the prize. The prize has been won. Instead, the goal is not to lose the prize.*

Was the apostle Paul a sports fan? At the least, he certainly understood athletic competition. In fact, he referred to competitive events like wrestling, fighting, shadowboxing, and "the games" in various epistles. He was particularly fond of comparing the Christian life to a race. For example, he wrote in Galatians 5:7, "You ran well. Who hindered you from obeying the truth?" And in 2 Timothy 4:7, "I have fought the good fight, I have finished the race, I have kept the faith."

Paul's reference to running a race would have been especially relevant for the Corinthians. Corinth was the site of the Isthmian Games, an athletic competition second in importance only to the Olympics. Yet, likening the Christian life to a race is also meaningful to us. Many of us have watched Olympic runners on television. Virtually all of us have run races; if not in athletic competition, then racing across a playground to claim a favorite swing, or racing across asphalt to get the last parking space.

The objective of racing is to win. In serious competition, winning requires training. Training involves discipline, self-control, commitment, proper diet, and strenuous effort. If this is true of an athletic event, it is certainly true of the Christian life. Thankfully, the race of faith differs in many ways from an Olympic race.

## God Gives the Crown

In an Olympic race, winning the crown depends on the

strength, stamina, and skill of the runner. But in the race of faith, winning the crown depends entirely on God—His strength, His commitment. He is the One who calls us to the starting-block and carries us over the finish line. As Paul wrote in Philippians 1:6, "being confident of this very thing, that He who has begun a good work in you will complete it until the day of Jesus Christ."

### The Crown is Won and Waiting

In an Olympic race, a crown is not given until won. But in the race of faith, the crown has already been won and is waiting for us. Jesus won the victory through His suffering, death, and resurrection. And we share in His victory through faith. We will wear the crown of life in eternity, but through faith we own it now in the present. Jesus said, "Most assuredly, I say to you, he who hears My word and believes in Him who sent Me *has* everlasting life, and shall not come into judgment, but *has* passed from death into life," John 5:24.

### Even Last Place is First Place

Paul wrote in 1 Corinthians 9:24, "Do you not know that those who run in a race all run, but one receives the prize?" This was the reality at the ancient Olympics. There were no gold, silver, and bronze medals; no first, second, and third-place finishes. A runner either won or lost, took first place or no place.

Yet, in the race of faith, even last place is first place. Everyone who crosses the finish line in faith will receive the same crown of life. To quote Jesus, "Be faithful until death, and I will give you the crown of life," Revelation 2:10.

### This Crown Will Last Forever

In antiquity, Olympic crowns were made of wild olive leaves. Many such crowns were no doubt wilting by the time the victors put them on. All that sacrifice, sweat, pain, and training for a crown that could never last. Even today, the longer-lasting medals awarded at the Olympics can still be lost, stolen, or broken. In fact, during the 2012 London Olympics, a Brazilian athlete broke his bronze medal while showering.

By contrast, the crown of life we will receive at the Lord's return will last for eternity. As Paul wrote, "Now they do it to obtain a perishable crown, but we for an imperishable crown," 1 Corinthians 9:25.

## Keeping Eyes on the Goal

When racing for the crown, we don't really compete against others. We compete against ourselves: New Man against the Old. Moreover, in the race of faith, the goal is not to win the prize. The prize has been won. Instead, the goal is not to lose the prize, as Paul wrote in 1 Corinthians 9:26-27, "Therefore I run thus: not with uncertainty. Thus I fight: not as one who beats the air. But I discipline my body and bring it into subjection, lest, when I have preached to others, I myself should become disqualified."

When I was a sophomore in high school and on the junior varsity basketball team, the coach put me into the varsity game for the final moments. I was elated. Somehow, the basketball bounced into my hands. It was my golden "Olympic Moment." Racing down the floor, I laid the ball perfectly into the basket. I turned. I jumped up and down. I shouted. I smiled at the cheering crowd, until I realized why the crowd was cheering. I'd shot the ball into the wrong basket, scoring two points for the other team. All the style, technique, and form in the world make no difference when your eyes are on the wrong goal.

At heart, 1 Corinthians 9:24-27 is about remembering the crown of life waiting for us, never taking that crown for granted or doing anything to jeopardize our receiving it. Instead, let's say with the apostle Paul: "I press toward the goal for the prize of the upward call of God in Christ Jesus," Philippians 3:14.

# Resolved, in Christ

Colossians 3:12-17

*Four resolutions for the New Year: "I resolve to dress better, sleep better, listen better, and undertake better—all in Jesus Christ."*

According to the Wall Street Journal, nearly half of all Americans make New Year's resolutions. And of these resolutions, 22% succeed and 78% fail. Of course, not all resolutions are important. But some are, like the resolve to lead God-pleasing lives.

Colossians 3:12-17 contains four important calls-to-action, and each one is an appropriate resolution for the New Year. We are to clothe ourselves with Christian attributes, verse 12; to let the peace of Christ rule in our hearts, verse 15; to let the word of Christ dwell in us richly, verse 16; and to do everything in the name of the Lord Jesus, verse 17.

However, these biblical resolutions are different from traditional New Year's resolutions. To begin with, Paul is not urging us to become something we are not—as is true of traditional resolutions. Instead, he is telling us to simply live up to the reality of who we are in Christ Jesus ,namely, "the elect of God, holy and beloved," Colossians 3:12.

Nor does Paul call upon us to pursue these resolutions alone—a certain recipe for failure. Rather, he tells us to do everything "in the name of the Lord Jesus, giving thanks to God the Father through Him," Colossians 3:17. Christ is the reason, the power, and the motivation for leading God-pleasing lives, as Paul reminds us in Philippians 4:13, "I can do all things through Christ who strengthens me." So then, we are resolved in Christ to lead godly lives.

**Resolved to "Dress" Better in Christ**

In Colossians 3:12, Paul urges us to clothe ourselves with Christian attributes: compassion, kindness, humility gentleness, patience, forbearance, forgiveness, and love. In fact, the act of "clothing" oneself is one of Paul's favorite metaphors, a metaphor he uses twelve times in seven epistles. For example, he says in Galatians 3:27, "For as many of you as were baptized into Christ have put on Christ."

Yet, unlike literal clothing, which can be changed to suit any circumstance, godly attributes are to be put on and left on. They reflect who we are in Christ. They are a *perfect fit* for our great salvation, and clearly identify us as the disciples of Christ. Jesus said in John 13:34-35, "A new commandment I give to you, that you love one another; as I have loved you, that you also love one another. By this all will know that you are My disciples, if you have love for one another."

**Resolved to Sleep Better in Christ**

One of the frightening aspects of any New Year is that we can't see into the future; not by a day, minute, or second. The uncertainty can make us worry; and the worry can cost us sleep. Yet, God *can* see into the future. Not only does He see our future, He controls it with the same love, purpose, and commitment that moved Him to send Jesus Christ into the world to be our Savior.

This is why Paul urges us to "let the peace of God rule in your hearts," Colossians 3:15. The peace that is from God. The peace that is found in Christ. This peace will govern our hearts, if we let it; if we give our problems and worries to God and trust Him to solve them. Isn't this what the Bible promises? Paul wrote in Philippians 4:6-7, "Be anxious for nothing, but in everything by prayer and supplication, with thanksgiving, let your requests be made known to God; and the peace of God, which surpasses all understanding, will guard your hearts and minds through Christ Jesus."

The Greek word Paul used for "rule" in Colossians 3:15

literally means "to umpire." Think of a baseball umpire. When problems come into our lives, the peace of Christ will tell them, "You're out!" When we begin to doubt God's love and faithfulness, the peace of Christ will tell us, "You're safe!"

### Resolved to Listen Better in Christ

It is no accident that, after urging us to let the peace of God rule our hearts, Paul urges us to "let the word of Christ dwell in you richly," Colossians 3:16. The peace, joy, and hope we so desperately want for our lives and loved ones only come through the Word of God.

Unfortunately, when we experience difficulties or convince ourselves that God has somehow let us down, we often turn away from the Bible and church. Yet, difficult times are the times in which we need to hear the Word of God the most. Contrary to popular opinion, we don't attend church to do something nice for God. Instead, we attend church to let God do something miraculous to us through His Word.

### Resolved to Undertake Better in Christ

Paul wrote, "And whatever you do in word and deed, do all in the name of the Lord Jesus, giving thanks to God the Father through Him," Colossians 3:17.

This is a fitting conclusion to Colossians 3:12-17, and a fitting summary of the Christian life. Whatever *you* do throughout your life; whether resolving to be more compassionate, kind, humble, gentle, patient, forbearing, forgiving, and loving; whether resolving to let the peace of God rule your heart, or to let the word of Christ dwell in you richly; whether resolving to be a better spouse or parent; or whether resolving to read the entire Bible, including the Old Testament, and even the Book of Leviticus—do it all in the name of the Lord Jesus. Do it in His power. Do it in His authority. Do it in conformity with His will, knowing "that your labor is not in vain in the Lord," 1 Corinthians 15:58.

# Running the Race
# with Perseverance

Hebrews 12:1-3

*Giving up may be the human way; but it is not the way of faith.*

The author of Hebrews wrote, "and let us run with endurance the race that is set before us," Hebrews 12:1. The Greek word for endurance, *UPOMONE*, literally means "to remain under," that is, having the ability to remain under heavy burdens and stressful situations without giving up or giving in. Where does this type of endurance or perseverance come from?

## Be Grateful You are Running the Race

Imagine receiving a call from the Olympic Committee. "We have a proposition for you," they say. "One of our long-distance runners can no longer compete. We'd like you to take his place at the next Olympics." How would you feel? Honored at first, then unworthy, then completely unqualified. "Well," you reply, "I'm not as young or as fast as I used to be. I've packed on a few pounds over the years. The only running I've done lately is from the sofa to the refrigerator."

In a far greater way, none of us were qualified to run the Christian race. God did not choose us to run the race of faith because we were talented, fast, strong, holy, full of good works, or worthy of His calling. In fact, until He called us to faith in Jesus Christ, we were running in the wrong direction, that is, running away from Him.

If we suffer in any way for our faith, as did the first readers of Hebrews, do we realize how blessed we are to have the gift of faith; how blessed we are to suffer for Christ's sake? Paul wrote in Philippians 1:29, "For to you it has been granted on behalf of Christ, not only to believe in Him, but also to suffer for His sake."

### Remember Who Is Directing Your Race

The Greek of Hebrews 12:1 is more literally "let us go on running the race being laid out for us." In other words, God is constantly customizing your Christian race to best serve your daily and eternal needs; strengthen your faith; and bring you safely across the finish line between time and eternity. Isn't this comforting?

Sometimes, running the Christian race hurts. In fact, the Greek word for "race," *AGON*, is the source of our English word *agony*. The obstacles hurt. The running hurts. The training hurts. But as any Olympic athlete will tell you, you cannot build muscle up without tearing it down. You cannot grow stronger without lifting heavy weights. God has a gymnasium, too, in which He strips away our pride and self-righteousness and "the sin which so easily ensnares us," Hebrews 12:1, and teaches us to rely solely on Jesus Christ.

The problems we encounter in life can be dreadful and painful. Yet, doesn't it comfort you to know that every obstacle and every step of your Christian race have been "marked out" by God; that every problem is under His complete direction, determination, and dominion?

### Turn to the Examples in Scripture

The first word in Hebrews 12:1, "therefore," points back to a long list of biblical characters in Hebrews 11: Abel, Noah, Abraham, Isaac, Jacob, Joseph, Moses, Gideon, Samson, and many others. When you tire in your race of faith, consider theirs. Are you weary of waiting for God to fulfill a promise? Abraham waited twenty years. Are you troubled by the time required to build a Christian congregation? Noah spent forty years building the ark. Do you feel imprisoned by personal circumstances? Joseph was unjustly imprisoned for years; and not for doing wrong, but for choosing right. Eventually, God made Joseph a ruler in Egypt.

When you feel like giving up, open your Bible and read the histories of these people of God: their tragedies and their triumphs. See them as the writer of Hebrews saw them—a vast cloud of witnesses, not spectators; filling an Olympic Stadium; and cheering you on in your Christian race. And what are they shouting? Not "Go! Go! Go!" Rather, "By faith! By faith! By faith!"

## Focus on Jesus Christ

"Let us run with endurance the race that is set before us, looking unto Jesus," Hebrews 12:1-2. The Greek word used for "looking," *APHORAO*, means to take our eyes off of every distraction—including our burdens, worries, problems, and disappointments—in order to focus exclusively on Jesus. Why is this important?

Remembering what Jesus endured—the suffering, the shame, the cross—will certainly help us endure our own trials and troubles. As explained in Hebrews 12:3, "For consider Him who endured such hostility from sinners against Himself, lest you become weary and discouraged in your souls."

But the encouragement is even more than this. When we remember what Jesus willingly endured to redeem us from our sins, we will have no reason to doubt His ability to understand our pains and sorrows, no reason to doubt His ability to keep our faith strong and our salvation safe, and no reason to doubt His ability to bring us safely across the finish line of the Christian race.

Jesus is the "author and finisher of our faith," Hebrews 12:2. Said another way, Jesus is both the starting block and finish line of the Christian race.

# The Alpha and the Omega

Revelation 1:4-8

*Jesus Christ is everything we need, from*
*A to Z.*

Scripture contains many names for God, and each one describes something important about His divine nature. For example, He is *ELOHIM*, the majestic God of Creation. He is *ADONAI*, the Lord God. He is *EL SHADDAI*, the Almighty God, and *YAVEH*, the eternally faithful God. These are not names that we chose for God, but names by which God revealed Himself to us. They are not merely forms of address, they are descriptions of God's attributes.

The Book of Revelation provides more than twenty names or titles for Jesus. Among them: Faithful Witness, Firstborn from the Dead, Son of Man, Son of God, Amen, Lamb, King of Kings and Lord of Lords. However, only in Revelation is Jesus called the ALPHA and the OMEGA.

In Revelation 1:8 Jesus says, "I am the Alpha and the Omega, the Beginning and the End." And in 1:11, "I am the Alpha and the Omega, the First and the Last." And in 22:13, "I am the Alpha and the Omega, the Beginning and the End, the First and the Last."

*Alpha* and *Omega* are the beginning and end, the first and last, letters of the Greek Alphabet; equivalent to our *A* and *Z*. But what does this name mean when applied to Jesus?

## Jesus Is Eternal

"Alpha and Omega," particularly with the explanation "First and Last," describes Jesus as eternal. As God the Son, He existed before all things and will endure eternally beyond all things. The author of Hebrews wrote of Jesus, "But You are the same, and Your years will not fail," Hebrews 1:12.

You and I cannot comprehend the eternity of God—that He has always existed; that He had no beginning and will have no end. Yet, at its simplest, *eternal* means "always there." And as our Alpha and Omega, Jesus is always there for us, always loving and forgiving, protecting and providing, always giving us God's Very Best, always inviting, "Come to Me, all you who labor and are heavy laden, and I will give you rest," Matthew 11:28.

## Jesus Is the Source of All Things

"Alpha and Omega," especially with the addition "Beginning and End," describes Jesus as the source of all things. He is the Creator Who carried out each of God the Father's "Let there be!" at the creation of the universe.

Paul wrote of Jesus in Colossians 1:16-17, "For by Him all things were created that are in heaven and that are on earth, visible and invisible, whether thrones or dominions or principalities or powers. All things were created through Him and for Him. And He is before all things, and in Him all things consist."

While you and I cannot grasp the infinite power and wisdom that God exerted in creation—the vastness of the universe and the complexities of life, these attributes of God give us great comfort. According to the Bible, God is exerting this same infinite power and infinite wisdom in our daily lives.

On this basis, Paul wrote in Romans 8:28, "And we know that all things work together for good to those who love God." And in Romans 8:31, "If God is for us, who can be against us?" Do the math. The answer is, no one and nothing can effectively oppose us, not with God's infinite wisdom and power at work in our lives.

## Jesus Is Our All-Sufficient Savior

You've heard advertisements from retailers who promise, "Come on down. We carry everything from A to Z." This same idea is contained in the name Alpha and Omega. Jesus

Christ is everything we need from A to Z. Or as beautifully expressed by the hymnist, "Just as I am, poor, wretched, blind; sight, riches, healing of the mind, yea, *all I need, in Thee to find*, O Lamb of God, I come, I come."

How comforting to know that every aspect of our salvation from A to Z has been perfectly accomplished through the blood and sacrifice of Jesus Christ. Nothing is missing. There is nothing left for us to do. As Paul wrote in Romans 8:1, "There is therefore now no condemnation to those who are in Christ Jesus." Or as stated so comfortingly in Revelation 1:5, "To Him who loved us and washed us from our sins in His own blood."

"I am the Alpha and the Omega," said Jesus. Don't simply rejoice in this knowledge. Live each day in its power.

# The Big Picture

Colossians 1:13-20

*It's not that our problems are too big. It's that our view of God is often too small.*

I have a picture of Jesus in my wallet. It's not a photograph or an artist's rendition. It's a word-picture of Jesus, as described in Colossians 1:13-20. I call this picture of Jesus the BIG PICTURE, big because it tells me precisely how BIG Jesus is—His big love, His big power, big grace, and big compassion. And I look at this picture of Jesus whenever I'm hurting, sad, or overwhelmed with problems. What does the BIG PICTURE tell us?

**Jesus Is True God**

As Jesus hung on the cross, a long parade of people relentlessly mocked Him. The religious leaders said, "He saved others; let Him save Himself." The Roman soldiers said, "If You are the king of the Jews, save Yourself." And then to add insult to injury, they nailed a sign on the cross which mockingly stated, THE KING OF THE JEWS. To the soldiers, this was a joke of cosmic proportion.

Even one of the malefactors crucified with Jesus mocked Him, saying, "Aren't You the Christ? Save Yourself and us." Yet, none of these unbelieving enemies of Jesus saw the BIG PICTURE, namely, that the Man who hung bleeding and dying on the cross was none other than God the Son—God in the flesh.

By the grace of God, you and I do see the BIG PICTURE; though we don't always apply it. If we did apply it, would we feel so powerless at times, so alone and adrift, so reluctant to undertake "this task" or improve "this relationship" or endure "this heartache"? It isn't that our problems are too big. It's that our view of God is often too small.

Are you facing insurmountable problems today—a serious illness, financial crisis, painful relationship? See the BIG PICTURE as Paul described it in Colossians 1:13-20. Paul, who declared of Jesus, "He is the image of the invisible God," 1:15, and, "For it pleased the Father that in Him all the fullness should dwell," 1:19, and later in 2:9, "For in Him dwells all the fullness of the Godhead bodily." See this BIG PICTURE, and then tell me that there is something, even one thing, that Jesus Christ cannot change, solve, heal, or accomplish in your life.

### Jesus Is Our Redeemer

Jesus atoned for our sins by His death on the cross. Yet, the world doesn't see it that way. From the worldly perspective, Christ's death was defeat, not victory.

Yet, when the Jews and Gentiles killed Jesus, thinking they had succeeded in their plan, the reality was that in the BIG PICTURE they were merely carrying out God's Plan of Redemption. As explained in Acts 4, "For truly against Your holy Servant Jesus, whom You anointed, both Herod and Pontius Pilate, with the Gentiles and the people of Israel, were gathered together to do *whatever Your hand and Your purpose determined before to be done.*"

There are dark hours in which we all feel the weight of our guilt, when an otherwise peaceful day is broken apart by the unexpected memory of a past sin, of the dreadful way we treated others, of the times we convinced ourselves that God didn't care about our behavior.

If you're in these dark hours, wondering how God could forgive you, stop, take a step back, and look at the BIG PICTURE—the limitless, unmerited forgiveness that is yours in Jesus Christ. As Paul wrote in Colossians 1:13-14, "He has delivered us from the power of darkness and conveyed us into the kingdom of the Son of His love, in whom we have redemption through His blood, the forgiveness of sins."

**Jesus Is in Control**

I know what "big pictures" you see on television. Wars. Riots. Natural disasters. Increasing hostility toward Christianity. Terrorism. Erosion of morals. Kim Jong-un with his nuclear missiles. Putin with his invasions. Assad with his chemical weapons. At times, our world, nation, and personal lives seem out of control. If you walked into a classroom and saw children dancing on their desks, laughing, screaming, and throwing erasers—no teachers in sight—you'd likely ask, "Who's in charge here?"

Yet, here, too, we need to look beyond the news footage to see the BIG PICTURE of Jesus Christ controlling all things. Notice how often Paul used the words "all things" in Colossians 1:13-20. Speaking of Christ, "For by Him all things were created," 1:16, and later in the same verse, "All things were created through Him and for Him." Then twice more in 1:17, "And He is before all things, and in Him all things consist." And again in 1:18, "that in all things He may have the preeminence." Finally, in 1:20, "and by Him to reconcile all things to Himself."

What is God telling us by this repetition? There is not a single thing in the universe or in your life that is outside of His control, from a distant galaxy to a blade of grass, from a molecule to a marriage, "whether thrones or dominions or principalities or powers," Colossians 1:16.

When your life seems out of control, don't read the news. Read the Bible. See the BIG PICTURE of Christ reigning supreme; indeed, reigning in such a gracious way that He will force even the worst circumstances to serve your best interests. This is not my promise, but His: "And we know that all things work together for good to those who love God, to those who are the called according to His purpose," Romans 8:28.

# The Facts of the Resurrection

1 Corinthians 15:1-11

*The Bible states plainly and unapologetically that Jesus Christ rose from the dead on Easter morning.*

The warning was clear. "Of every tree of the garden you may freely eat; but of the tree of the knowledge of good and evil you shall not eat, for in the day that you eat of it you shall surely die," Genesis 2:16-17. In Hebrew "you shall surely die" is more literally "dying you shall die." With the fall into sin, mankind's existence became a dead, dying existence.

And what words better describe our world than *death* and *dying*? Globally, there are 105 deaths each minute, 6,316 deaths each hour, 150,600 deaths each day, and 55.3 million deaths each year. Imagine how many industries are related to death: funeral, medical, insurance, mental health, forensics, armed forces, and more. Even our entertainment industry is riddled with death. By the time a child has finished elementary school, he or she will have witnessed eight thousand murders on television.

But enough statistics about death. How has death impacted you personally? How many funerals have you attended? How many obituaries have you read? How many loved ones have you lost: grandparents, parents, children, friends? Even the death of a beloved family pet can cause severe grief. Yet, nowhere does the resurrection of Jesus Christ have more meaning than amid the harsh realities of death and dying. And to know the power of Christ's resurrection, and to live in that power, we must know, believe, and apply the facts of the resurrection. What are the facts?

## Jesus Rose from the Dead

The historical Jesus of Nazareth, who "was conceived by

the Holy Spirit, born of the Virgin Mary, suffered under Pontius Pilate, was crucified, dead, and buried"—this Jesus rose triumphantly from the grave on the first Easter morning. Does the world believe this? No. The world assigns the resurrection of Jesus no more credibility than the Easter Bunny.

But in God's inspired Word, the suffering, death, and resurrection of Jesus are not myth; they are divine fact. The resurrection is referenced in twenty-two of the twenty-seven books in the New Testament. All four gospels—Matthew, Mark, Luke, and John—not only record the fact of the resurrection; but also many resurrection appearances in which the risen Jesus walked, talked, ate, and in one instance, even cooked breakfast for His disciples on the shore of Lake Galilee. Paul wrote that the risen Jesus was witnessed "by over five hundred brethren at once," 1 Corinthians 15:6.

The Bible states plainly and unapologetically that Jesus Christ rose from the dead. This is a fact.

**Jesus Was Who He claimed to Be**

Some insist that Jesus never claimed to be God. This is blatantly untrue. In John 8, for example, Jesus told the unbelieving Jews, "Most assuredly, I say to you, before Abraham was, I AM." This was not poor sentence construction on the part of Jesus. When He said, "I AM," He was claiming the great name of *YAVEH* or Jehovah for Himself. *YAVEH* is a Hebrew verb meaning "I AM." It was the same as saying, "I am the eternal God." That the Jews understood this claim is evident from their immediate attempt to stone Jesus for blasphemy.

In John 10:30 Jesus said, "I and My Father are one." One in essence. One in majesty. One in power and glory. And here, too, the Jews attempted to stone Jesus for blasphemy for claiming to be God.

When the pompous high priest demanded of Jesus, "I put You under oath by the living God: Tell us if You are the

Christ, the Son of God!" Jesus replied, "It is as you said," Matthew 26:63-64.

When God the Father raised Jesus from the dead, He vindicated every claim Jesus made about Himself. More than anything else—the miracles, the teaching—the resurrection of Jesus Christ proved that He was exactly Who He claimed to be: God the Son, God our Savior.

### Jesus Did What He Came to Do

Everything Jesus did, said, and suffered in our place would be meaningless without His resurrection, just as Good Friday would be meaningless without Easter Sunday. This is why Paul wrote in 1 Corinthians 15:17, "And if Christ is not risen, your faith is futile; you are still in your sins!"

But when God the Father raised Jesus from the dead, He was declaring in unmistakable terms that He had accepted the atonement Jesus made for our sins, that what Jesus proclaimed on the cross—"It is finished!"—was in fact true. In resurrecting Jesus, God the Father was assuring each of us, "No matter who you are, what you've done, where you've been, or how long you've been away, I have redeemed you through My Son. And the proof is in His resurrection."

### Jesus Told the Truth

Each time Jesus forewarned His disciples of His suffering and death, He also promised His resurrection. Yet, on the first Easter, what were His disciples doing? Not celebrating their living Lord, but mourning their dead Savior. Many were hiding behind locked doors. The women who hurried to the cemetery wondered, "Who will roll away the stone?" Mary Magdalene mistook the risen Christ for the cemetery caretaker. Peter and John likely equated the empty tomb with body theft instead of bodily resurrection. Thomas refused to accept Christ's resurrection as factual without forensic evidence. The two disciples shuffling sadly along Emmaus Road lamented of Jesus, "We thought He was the One."

Significantly, when Jesus appeared to the Emmaus disciples, He did not chide them for failing to recognize Him, but for failing to recognize the truth of the Scriptures—the same Scriptures we have in our possession. "O foolish ones," said Jesus, "and slow of heart to believe in all that the prophets have spoken!" Luke 24:25. Paul wrote in 1 Corinthians 15:3-4 that "Christ died for our sins *according to the Scriptures*, and that He was buried, and that He rose again the third day *according to the Scriptures*."

God keeps His word, every letter, every syllable. And the resurrection is the proof.

## Because Jesus Lives, We Will Live Too

On Easter, we are often reminded of those we have loved and lost. Are there tears? Yes. But amid the tears and loss, there is also a sense of overwhelming victory. For the same Jesus who rose triumphantly that first Easter also declared in John 14, "Because I live, you will live also." You and I will rise from the dead. You and I will be reunited with those Christian loved ones we lost. These glorious realities are guaranteed by Christ's resurrection.

The apostle Paul wrote in the closing words of 1 Corinthians 15 (referring to Isaiah 25:8), "'O Death, where is your sting? O Hades, where is your victory?' The sting of death is sin, and the strength of sin is the law. But thanks be to God, who gives us the victory through our Lord Jesus Christ. Therefore, my beloved brethren, be steadfast, immovable, always abounding in the work of the Lord, knowing that your labor is not in vain in the Lord."

How do we know? Because Jesus is alive. And that is a fact.

# The Gibeonite Deception

Joshua 9:3-15

*Decisions have consequences. "Oh, how different my life would be today if only I had. . ."*

After forty years of wilderness wanderings, the Israelites finally entered the Promised Land to conquer and possess it. Cities fell, kings fled, nations trembled; not because of Israel's size, strength or military prowess, but because of Israel's God. As Joshua later reminded the Israelites: "You have seen all that the LORD your God has done to all these nations because of you, for the LORD your God is He who has fought for you," Joshua 23:3.

Amid these victories, however, a single event occurred which impacted the Israelites for the next four centuries, from the time of Joshua to the time of King David and King Solomon. This event was the so-called Gibeonite Deception.

Gibeon was built on a hill six miles northwest of Jerusalem. Its original inhabitants were Amorites and Hivites, who fell under the condemnation of Deuteronomy 7: "When the LORD your God brings you into the land which you go to possess, and has cast out many nations before you, the Hittites and the Girgashites and the Amorites and the Canaanites and the Perizzites and the Hivites and the Jebusites, seven nations greater and mightier than you, and when the LORD your God delivers them over to you, you shall conquer them and *utterly destroy* them. You shall make no covenant with them nor show mercy to them."

Yet, the Israelites did make a treaty with the Gibeonites, not knowingly, but carelessly. Posing as ambassadors from a distant land, the Gibeonites tricked the Israelites into making a peace treaty with them. As a result of this treaty, the Israelites were compelled to protect the Gibeonites instead of destroying them. Why was the Gibeonite Deception so successful? Because Joshua and the Israelites "did not ask counsel of the LORD," Joshua 9:14.

There is a powerful lesson here for all of us: Seek God's counsel in every aspect of life. And how do we seek God's counsel? Through prayer and by turning to God's Word.

## Decisions Have Consequences

Joshua's failure to consult God when dealing with the Gibeonites resulted in four hundred years of consequences: wars, blood, cost, pain, suffering, grief, death, and even a famine.

Almost immediately, as a result of that peace treaty, the Israelites were required to protect the Gibeonites from five Amorite armies. But four centuries later, because of the same treaty, King David was forced to kill seven sons of King Saul due to Saul's bloody persecution of the Gibeonites. In fact, until David avenged the Gibeonites, God sent a famine on the land of Israel. God explained, "It is because of Saul and his bloodthirsty house, because he killed the Gibeonites," 2 Samuel 21:1.

Decisions have consequences. "Oh, how different my life would be today if only I had. . ." What? How would you complete that sentence? "If only I had taken that job." "If only I had paid more attention to my spouse." "If only I had overcome that temptation." Perhaps the truer sentence would be "How different my life would be today if only I had consulted God."

## Deception Is Everywhere

Though Joshua was the leader of the Israelites, he was still fooled by the Gibeonite Deception. Yet, he would not have been deceived if only he had consulted God. The same is true of us.

Deception is all around us. The world with its glamor and glittering promises is a deceiver. The devil is a deceiver and seducer who wants to destroy our faith in Jesus by spouting lies and twisting truths. As sinful human beings, we have an amazing capacity to deceive ourselves into believing that right is wrong and wrong is right, that a little worldliness has no impact on godliness, and that God cares nothing about our behavior as long as we attend church on Sunday.

Now, more than ever, we need to seek God's counsel and immerse ourselves in God's Word, so that we are not deceived by the devil, the world, our own sinful nature, and false teachers; but rather, remain steadfast in God's truth. "Beloved," wrote John, "do not believe every spirit, but test the spirits, whether they are of God; because many false prophets have gone out into the world," 1 John 4:1.

When we have important decisions to make and endeavors to undertake, let's remember these words of the hymnist:

"With the Lord begin thy task,
Jesus will direct it;
For His aid and counsel ask,
Jesus will perfect it.
Every morn with Jesus rise,
And when day is ended,
In His name then close thine eyes;
Be to Him commended."

# The Great Commission

Matthew 28:18-20

*Is the work of the Christian Church to go out or bring in? Is it to make disciples or make members?*

Two thousand years ago, the Lord Jesus gave His disciples a great responsibility. He said, "All authority has been given to Me in heaven and on earth. Go, therefore and make disciples of all the nations, baptizing them in the name of the Father and of the Son and of the Holy Spirit, teaching them to observe all things that I have commanded you; and lo, I am with you always, even to the end of the age," Matthew 28:18-20. These words of Jesus are often called the Great Commission. But what makes the Great Commission so great?

**Great Power**

On their own, the first disciples were not equipped to carry out the Great Commission. None were trained missionaries. None held theological degrees. Most of the original disciples were simple, unschooled Galilean fishermen, who knew more about mending broken nets than mending broken hearts. They had no operating budget, no pews, no printed Bibles or hymnals. They met in homes, not cathedrals.

Paul wrote to the Corinthians, "For you see your calling, brethren, that not many wise according to the flesh, not many mighty, not many noble, are called," 1 Corinthians 1:26. Instead, Christ gave His Great Commission to ordinary Christians. And what Christ commanded His people to do, He also empowered them to do.

Most Christians can recite the Great Commission: "Go therefore and make disciples of all the nations. . . ." But far too often, as individuals and congregations, in meetings and planning, we neglect to include Matthew 28:18. Before ever sending His disciples out to proclaim the gospel, Jesus first reminded them, "All authority has been given to Me in heaven and on earth." The Greek word translated as "authority," *EXOUSIA*, also means power. All power. All authority. Remember this when you have an opportunity to tell a friend about Christ, or to witness to a coworker, or to canvass a neighborhood. Don't think, "I don't know if I can do this or say that." Think, "I have been sent here by Jesus. I speak and act in His name, by His authority."

### Great Work

But what is the great work of the Christian Church? Is it to form political action committees, or to instigate social reform, or to feed the hungry? Clearly, God wants us to help others in need. Paul wrote in Galatians 6:10, "Therefore, as we have opportunity, let us do good to all, especially to those who are of the household of faith." Yet, this is not the great work of the Christian Church.

When defining the great work of the Great Commission, Jesus used four important verbs: GO, DISCIPLE, BAPTIZE, and TEACH. Our responsibility is to go out. It is the Spirit of God's responsibility to bring in. And He does His great work through the Holy Scriptures. This is why Jesus equated making disciples with administering the Means of Grace; specifically, baptizing and teaching. So, the Christian Church is to be a TEACHING Church, not an entertaining Church.

But what should we teach? Should we teach those Scriptures that suit our mood or fall within the boundaries of political correctness? Should we omit words like *sin*, *guilt*, and *condemnation*? Should we tone down the exclusivity of Christ's words, "I am the way, the truth, and the life. No one comes to the Father except through me," John 14:6? Should we eliminate the cross from our church buildings, sermons, hymnals, and Bibles?

Sadly, many churches today take this approach to the Great Commission. Yet, when they do, they are not following

Christ's mandate, but rather their own. They are not focusing on making disciples, but on making members. And this is wrong.

In His Great Commission, Jesus said, "teaching them to observe all things that I have commanded you," Matthew 28:20. All things. All Scripture. All about God. All about law and gospel. All about marriage, ministry, fellowship, creation, the Lord's Supper, and baptism. All about who we are by nature, and how we are saved by grace.

## Great Promise

Throughout the Great Commission, Jesus used the word *all* four times: "all authority," verse 18; "all the nations," verse 19; "all things," verse 20; and also in verse 20, "And lo, I am with you always, even to the end of the age." *LO* is an abbreviation for *LOOK*. Look at this, look at Christ, whenever you feel small, overwhelmed, or useless; whether as a Christian individual or Christian congregation.

"I am with you always." Can you think of a more comforting promise? Jesus is always with us, in life and death, amid joy and heartbreak. And when we step through the door of our home or church in answer to His "go therefore and make disciples of all the nations," Jesus Christ always steps through the door with us.

# The Little Things of Christmas

Micah 5:1-5

*"Big" is such a part of Christmas mentality, many find it difficult to equate a little Christmas with a merry Christmas.*

Much of what we associate with Christmas is BIG. Big excitement. Big Christmas trees. Big family gatherings. Big meals. Big crowds. Big traffic jams. Big presents. *Mom, why did he get the big present?* And once Christmas has passed, big credit card bills from all the big spending.

BIG is such a part of Christmas mentality, many find it difficult to equate a little Christmas with a merry Christmas. When the song "Have Yourself a Merry Little Christmas" was written for the 1944 movie *Meet Me in St. Louis*, Judy Garland refused to sing the original lyrics because, as she explained, "They're too sad. People will think me a monster." A monster, presumably, for suggesting that a little Christmas could be a merry Christmas.

Yet, so much about the Christmas Narrative in Scripture is about little things—some little in size, all little in the sense of lowliness. Nor should this surprise us. The apostle Paul wrote in 1 Corinthians 1:27-29, "But God has chosen the foolish things of the world to shame the wise, and God has chosen the weak things of the world to put to shame the things which are mighty; and the base things of the world and the things which are despised God has chosen, and the things which are not, to bring to nothing the things that are, that no flesh should glory in His presence."

## The Little People
Consider all the little, lowly people of the First Christmas:

Mary, a lowly virgin, chosen by God to be the mother of the Messiah. Joseph, a lowly carpenter, chosen by God to be the adoptive father of Jesus. Lowly shepherds, chosen by God to hear the first announcement of the Savior's birth. Shepherds were poor, uneducated, often despised, and prohibited from testifying in court. Yet, God chose lowly shepherds to be the first to testify about the birth of His Son. The shepherds "made widely known the saying which was told them concerning this Child," Luke 2:17.

At times, all of us feel too little to accomplish God-pleasing tasks. Abraham said, "I'm too old." Jeremiah said, "I'm too young." Moses said, "I can't speak well." Elijah hid in a cave. Jonah jumped ship. But these human inadequacies did not prevent God from accomplishing His purposes. In fact, through such littleness God displayed His strength. This is one of the lessons of Christmas.

## The Little Places

The prophet Micah wrote: "But you, Bethlehem Ephrathah, though you are little among the thousands of Judah," Micah 5:2. Bethlehem was where Jacob buried his wife Rachel; where Naomi, the mother-in-law of Ruth, lived; where Ruth met and married Boaz; where David was anointed king; where Jesus Christ was born; where shepherds heard the good news of Christ's birth; where the wise men found Jesus; and where Herod slaughtered all male children two years old and younger.

Yet, despite its long biblical history, Bethlehem was a very small place—too little to be included in the list of Israelite towns with a population of at least one thousand; that is, "the thousands of Judah." Yet, as God proclaimed, out of little Bethlehem "shall come forth to Me the One to be Ruler in Israel, whose goings forth are from of old, from everlasting," Micah 5:2.

Startling, isn't it? The long-promised Savior was not born in Jerusalem or any of the other large and prosperous Israelite cities, or even in the world capital of Rome. Instead, He was born in the littleness and nothingness of Bethlehem. And in this little place God fulfilled His big promise to save lost humanity.

Sometimes, we feel embarrassed when attending a little church; embarrassed that all we have to share with the world is the old family Bible, with its wrinkled cover and dog-earred pages and underlined verses. Have we forgotten? The Bible is the almighty power of God and the means through which the Holy Spirit calls lost and condemned sinners to repentance and faith in Jesus Christ. God uses little places and seemingly little means to accomplish big things. This, too, is a lesson of Christmas.

## The Little Baby

Of all the little things of Christmas, what was littler or humbler than the newborn Child Who was placed in a manger and wrapped in swaddling clothes? Yet, He was none other than the almighty Son of God—God, who came to us as a Baby, so that we would not fear Him. God, who shared in our humanity to atone for our sins, and so that you and I could never rightly say, "God, You don't understand me. You don't know what I'm going through." Yes, He does know and understand, because He Himself went through it and overcame it. And what big things God accomplished through that lowly birth.

If you feel sad or lonely today, if you feel little, insignificant, or unwanted, then this message is for you: "Do not be afraid, for behold, I bring you good tidings of great joy which will be to all people. For there is born to you this day in the city of David a Savior, who is Christ the Lord," Luke 2:10-11.

# The Right Foundation

Matthew 7:15-29

*The most important part of a house is its foundation. And if this is true of a building, it is certainly true of our lives.*

We seldom think about the foundation of a house. Yet, the foundation is the most important part of a house because every other component of the house depends on the foundation: floors, walls, ceiling, and roof. A foundation not only holds a house up, it holds a house firmly in place. Which part of a house is built first? Which part bears the entire weight? Which part provides underlying strength and stability? The foundation.

Obviously, everything depends on having the right foundation. And if this is true of your house, it is even truer of your life. In Matthew 7:15-29, Jesus teaches us the importance of building our lives on the right foundation; and that right foundation is the eternal, immovable, and indestructible foundation of His Word.

### Everyone Is a Builder

Each of us is a builder. We are constantly building our lives, hopes, and relationships on some kind of foundation. The only questions are: "What is that foundation?" "How strong is it?" "How long will it last?" "How much weight can it carry?" And as parents, grandparents, siblings, and friends, we also help build the lives of others. That is a sobering thought, isn't it?

### Only Two Types of Foundation

From the biblical perspective, there are but two

foundations for life: the Word of God, and everything else. Does it matter which foundation we use? Some say no. Believe in Jesus or believe in yourself. Believe in Christ or believe in Buddha. Different religions are just different avenues to the same divine place. True? Absolutely not. And if the words of Jesus in John 14:6 aren't enough—"I am the way, the truth, and the life. No one comes to the Father except through Me"—consider the outcome of the wise and foolish builders in Matthew 7.

The two houses in Christ's parable faced the same storm, but only one house stood while the other collapsed in ruins. What made the difference? Not the house, builder, or storm, but having the right foundation.

## Preparing for Storms

Storms are inevitable in life. Jesus did not mention a thirty-percent chance of rain or the possibility of afternoon thunderstorms. He said, "and the rain descended, the floods came, and the winds blew and beat on that house," Matthew 7:25, 27. The use of the plural in these verses implies intense, numerous storms. Floods. Winds.

Therefore, the time to prepare for storms is now. In the *Parable of the Wise and Foolish Builders* the only house that survived the storm "was founded on the rock," Matthew 7:25. But an even more literal translation of this verse is that the house "had been founded on the rock," that is, the foundation of that house, that life, had been laid long before the storm arrived.

In 1992, Hurricane Andrew destroyed thousands of homes in southern Florida. Yet, in an area where the wreckage resembled a war zone, one house remained standing, still firmly anchored to its foundation. When a reporter asked the homeowner why his house had survived, he replied, "I built this house myself. I also built it according to the Florida State Building Code. When the code called for 2x6 roof trusses, I used 2x6 roof trusses. I was told that a house built according to code could withstand a hurricane. And it did."

Build the foundation of your life on Jesus Christ and His Word, and you will never be disappointed. His building code comes with an iron-clad guarantee. "Behold, I lay in Zion a chief cornerstone, elect, precious, and he who believes on Him will by no means be put to shame," 1 Peter 2:6.

As the hymnist has written: "On Christ the solid Rock I stand; all other ground is sinking sand."

# The Wisdom of God

1 Corinthians 2:6-13

*King Solomon was wealthy, prominent, and powerful. Yet, what he wanted most for his children was wisdom from God.*

As parents, we want the best for our children. Understandably, perhaps, we often associate the best with material needs: food, clothing, shelter, education, career, happy marriage, long life. Yet, even with these amenities we wonder, "Did I do enough? Did I teach my children the right things? Did I give them what they need to stay level-headed amid success and hopeful amid heartache?" We ask these questions not only because we love our children, but because we've learned that there are some things in life, indeed, the most important things, that fame, fortune, and power cannot obtain.

King Solomon was one of the wisest, wealthiest, and most powerful men ever to live. Under his leadership, the kingdom of Israel reached its zenith and enjoyed forty years of prosperity and peace. Yet, Solomon, who could have given his children anything, most wanted them to have one thing; namely, wisdom from God. He wrote in Proverbs 2:6, "For the LORD gives wisdom; from His mouth come knowledge and understanding."

The apostle Paul wanted his readers to have the same wisdom from God. In 1 Corinthians 2:6-13 he explained the difference between human wisdom and God's wisdom.

### God's Wisdom Is Absolute

How many times have you heard an expert call something good, and then a short time later call the same thing bad? If human wisdom cannot be trusted with temporal outcomes, dare we trust it for eternal ones?

God's wisdom is absolute. His wisdom never changes because He never changes. "For I am the LORD, I do not change," is the promise of Malachi 3:6. God is never for us one day and against us the next. He is never faithless, loveless, capricious, sleepy, or moody. His word, will, and wisdom are as unchanging as He is. This means that His solution to our real-life problems never changes. And the solution is always Jesus Christ.

With God, there is never a doubt about how He views sin or how we are saved. "For the wages of sin is death, but the gift of God is eternal life in Christ Jesus our Lord," Romans 6:23.

### God's Wisdom Is Truthful

Human wisdom has benefits: scientific discoveries, technological advances, medical breakthroughs. Yet, when faced with life's most important questions—"Who am I?" "Where did I come from?" "Why am I here?" "What is my purpose?" "What is truth?" "Is there a God?" "How am I saved?" "What happens to me when I die?"—human wisdom has no answers. It is severely limited and frequently destructive.

This is what Paul meant when he wrote that the wisdom and rulers of this age "are coming to nothing," 1 Corinthians 2:6. Human wisdom often leads to nothing, and at times to far worse. How many people followed the so-called wisdom of Jim Jones to their deaths? The world is full of false wisdom and false messiahs.

By contrast, God's wisdom is always truthful, always powerful, and always redemptive. And that wisdom always presents Jesus Christ as the Answer to life's questions and problems. As Paul wrote in 1 Corinthians 1:30, "But of Him you are in Christ Jesus, who became for us WISDOM from God—and righteousness and sanctification and redemption."

**God's Wisdom Is Revealed**

I enjoy watching various programs on the Discovery, Learning, and History Channels. The photography is often spectacular, the subject-matter intriguing: the miracle of birth, the complexities of the human body, the vastness and grandeur of the universe. As I watch, I think, "O LORD, how manifold are Your works! In wisdom You have made them all," Psalm 104:24.

Then, near the end of the program, such wonders are inevitably attributed to the blind, random chance of evolution. It's all I can do to keep from hurling a shoe at the TV set. Instead, I stand and shout at it. "How can you say that?" I demand of the narrator. "How can you watch the same documentary I watched and arrive at such a different conclusion?"

But the answer, of course, is found in 1 Corinthians 2:9-10 (referring to Isaiah 64:4), "'Eye has not seen, nor ear heard, nor have entered into the heart of man the things which God has prepared for those who love Him.' But God has revealed them to us through His Spirit." For this revelation of the Spirit you and I should praise God every day. For without Him, we would not accept God's wisdom. We would not embrace Jesus Christ as our Lord and Savior.

In Proverbs 22:6 Solomon wrote, "Train up a child in the way he should go, and when he is old he will not depart from it." Comforting words. But there is another way to translate the Hebrew of this verse which I find even more comforting: "Train up a child in the way he should go, and when he is old it will not depart from him." In other words, God will remain faithful. God's wisdom will always be there, waiting, working, available, absolute.

So, let's teach our children the wisdom of God. That way, when the time comes for them to pack the car and leave home—and we stand in the driveway, teary-eyed and fiercely waving—we will know that we taught them the right thing: the wisdom from God.

# Things are Looking Up

Acts 1:1-11

*The ascension of Jesus Christ into heaven gives us every reason to look up in hope.*

Recently, I had a strange dream. I dreamt I was back on the campus of Immanuel Lutheran College in Eau Claire, Wisconsin, visiting with old classmates. As we talked, a group of young people filed past, smiling and waving. I realized almost immediately that I was one of those young people, looking as I had in high school. "Hey," I told one old friend, "see that guy over there? That's me." I waved at myself. The young me—trim, unwrinkled, with a full head of hair—waved back, then disappeared into the gray mist of my subconscious.

I didn't need a psychology degree to interpret my dream. The old me waving goodbye to the young me was symbolic of passing time and change. Goodbye, youth. Hello, age. I awoke from that dream feeling old, melancholy, and missing the young me. But then I began to wonder, "Should I be feeling so down, when our ascended Savior is living, interceding, and reigning at the right hand of God the Father?"

Many view the ascension of Jesus as if it were no more than a historical footnote to the work of redemption. But this is wrong. The ascension was and is of enormous significance. This is why Jesus Himself led His disciples to the site of the ascension. He wanted them to witness it, not so that they would remain on the Mount of Olives, staring indecisively into the clouds, but rather, so that they would return to their homes, families, jobs, and ministries with great joy. "And they worshiped Him, and returned to Jerusalem with great joy," Luke 24:52.

## Completion

When Jesus died on the cross, He atoned for *all* of our sins. "It is finished!" He said in John 19:30. The Greek word for *finished*, *TETELESTAI*, was actually a financial term used to mark transactions as PAID IN FULL. God the Father marked our salvation "paid in full" when He raised Jesus from the dead and seated Jesus at His right hand in heaven.

In the Apostles' Creed we confess, "He ascended into heaven." This is true. But the ascension was not only some action that Jesus did; it was also something done to Jesus. According to Acts 1:9, "Now when He had spoken these things, while they watched, He was taken up, and a cloud received Him out of their sight."

Note carefully. *Jesus was taken up*. He did not return to heaven on His own. He was returned to heaven by God the Father, because the work of redemption was entirely done. And this means that there is entirely nothing that we can do, or need to do, in order to be saved other than to trust in Jesus as our Savior.

The most important question we can ask in life is not "How can I become rich?" or "How can I live to be one hundred?" No, the most important question is the one asked by the trembling jailer at Philippi, "Sirs, what must I do to be saved?" To which Paul and Silas replied, "Believe on the Lord Jesus Christ, and you *will* be saved, you and your household," Acts 16:30-31. No matter what else is happening in our lives, our complete salvation in Christ should move us to say with joy and confidence: "Things are looking up."

## Dominion

As a child, I often puzzled over these words of the Apostles' Creed, "He ascended into heaven, and sits on the right hand of God the Father Almighty." Frankly, sitting on the Father's hand sounded uncomfortable. And why was Jesus sitting anyway? Was He tired, indifferent, on vacation?

Of course, Christ's "sitting" at the right hand of the Father has nothing to do with resting and everything to do with ruling. Even today we associate sitting and chairs with positions of authority: sitting presidents, county seats, chairmanships.

When Jesus ascended into heaven, He didn't just go to a place, He assumed a position of all authority and all power over the world, His Church, and our lives. This was one of the *visual* lessons of the ascension. The disciples were to equate Christ's "going up" with His "presiding over" as the Most High God.

The world may not always look as if it is under Christ's control. Nevertheless, it is. Instead of focusing on the daily headlines or nightly news, we should be focusing on Paul's words to the Philippians concerning the sovereignty of Christ: "Therefore God also has highly exalted Him and given Him the name which is above every name, that at the name of Jesus every knee should bow, of those in heaven, and of those on earth, and of those under the earth, and that every tongue should confess that Jesus Christ is Lord, to the glory of God the Father," Philippians 2:9-11.

Think about that. The name of JESUS is above every other name: Illness, Catastrophe, Financial Difficulty, Troubled Marriage. "All authority has been given to Me in heaven and on earth," said Jesus in Matthew 28:18, shortly before sending His little congregation of believers out to evangelize the world.

Yes, I may be aging, but Jesus is in control. I may be sick, but Jesus is in control. I may be worried about the state of our nation or the faith of my children, but Jesus is in control. Can you see why "things are looking up"?

## Intercession

As our ascended Lord, Jesus lives eternally to intercede for us. Paul wrote in Romans 8, "Who shall bring a charge against God's elect? It is God who justifies. Who is he who condemns? It is Christ who died, and furthermore is also risen, who is even at the right hand of God, who also makes intercession for us."

I'm reminded of the cherished Easter hymn, "He lives to bless me with His love, He lives to plead for me above." Is there anything more comforting than the knowledge that the One who is interceding for us also shared in our humanity, sorrows, and problems? You and I can never rightfully say, "God doesn't know what I'm going through." Yes, He does. He went through it in the Person of Jesus Christ.

As Jesus ascended into heaven, He raised His two hands and blessed His disciples—the two hands which will forever bear the marks of His love, grace, and crucifixion. Consider those two hands governing the world, governing the Christian Church, and governing every aspect of your life. You'll know why "things are looking up".

# Two Trees, Two Histories

Romans 5:12-19

*Many churches today are more focused on what people want to hear than on what they need to hear. What they need to hear is that we are sinful by nature and saved by grace.*

The apostle Paul warned of a time when people "will not endure sound doctrine, but according to their own desires, because they have itching ears, they will heap up for themselves teachers; and they will turn their ears away from the truth, and be turned aside to fables," 2 Timothy 4:3-4.

Sadly, that time came early to the Christian Church, and it is prevalent in our own age. Today, many churches have stopped talking about sin. Or if sin is mentioned, it is often trivialized—like the popular TV preacher who, during an Easter worship service, compared sin to "bad breath" and Jesus Christ to a "breath mint."

The Bible, however, never trivializes sin. In fact, it mentions the word *sin* and its synonyms more than 2,500 times. Why? It is impossible to see the need for a personal Savior without seeing the reality of personal sin. Jesus said in Mark 2:17, "Those who are well have no need of a physician, but those who are sick. I did not come to call the righteous, but sinners to repentance."

In Romans 5:12-19 the apostle Paul shows the link between sin and salvation; the first Adam and the Second Adam, Jesus Christ; the tree in Eden and the tree on Calvary.

## The Tree in Eden

There were, of course, two important trees in the center of Eden—the center, because they were central to humanity's relationship with God. One was the Tree of Life, and the other was the Tree of the Knowledge of Good and Evil. God told Adam, "Of every tree of the garden you may freely eat; but of the tree of the knowledge of good and evil you shall not eat, for in the day that you eat of it you shall surely die," Genesis 2:16-17. The Hebrew is literally "dying you shall die." Man's existence would become a dying existence, an existence characterized by death and ending in death.

When this prohibition was given, Adam and Eve were perfect, created in the image of God. They knew God. They knew themselves. They knew which tree was the right tree. There was nothing in them to make them desire the wrong tree. Yet, we know which tree they selected, and we can still see the tragic consequences of their choice: death and dying.

Why is there death? Why is there disease? Why is the natural tendency of everything physical in the universe, from packaged meat to distant galaxies, to decay instead of evolve? Why are there brutal acts of terrorism and unspeakable crimes? Why does even an abundance of wealth leave people feeling empty? Why do humans despise God or deny His existence?

That which science and human philosophy cannot answer, the Bible does. Everything wrong, shameful, violent, and destructive in our world originated with a single tree and single event in the Garden of Eden: "So when the woman saw that the tree was good for food, that it was pleasant to the eyes, and a tree desirable to make one wise, she took of its fruit and ate. She also gave to her husband with her, and he ate," Genesis 3:6.

In this single act of disobedience, the sin of Adam and Eve became our sin; their death, our death; their history, our history; and their sad future, our future.

One of the most popular programs on TV today is *The Walking Dead*, a series about animated corpses roaming the globe and devouring the living. There are no zombies, of course. However, according to Scripture, there are "the walking dead." Paul wrote in Ephesians 2:1-2, "And you He made alive, who were dead in trespasses and sins, in which you once walked." Dead and walking. Dead to God. Incapable of even the slightest spark of spiritual life.

This is the reality of sin. And therefore, to compare sin to bad breath, to teach people that they can save themselves through good deeds, to refuse to talk about sin in worship services—these things demonstrate a gross misunderstanding of sin, and the desire of some teachers to "scratch itching ears." Personal sin is why we so desperately need Jesus Christ as our personal Savior.

## The Tree on Calvary

It was no accident that Jesus died on a cross, a cruel tool of execution made from wood, taken *from a tree*. It was no accident that Jesus wore a crown of thorns—thorns which symbolized the curse, frustration, and meaninglessness that befell Man and Man's World through the fall into sin. "Cursed is the ground for your sake," God told Adam. "In toil you shall eat of it all the days of your life. Both thorns and thistles it shall bring forth for you," Genesis 3:17-18.

In Eden we were overcome at a tree. On Calvary Jesus overcame by a tree. In Eden we were cursed. On Calvary Jesus became our curse and atoned for it with His own blood. That which Jesus accomplished through the tree on Calvary has given us a far different history and a far different future than the death and condemnation that came through the tree in Eden.

Paul outlined these wondrous differences in Romans 5:12-19. Adam brought sin; Jesus brought salvation. Adam's disobedience brought death to all; Christ's sacrifice brought forgiveness for all. Indeed, on the cross Jesus atoned for every sin that has ever been committed or ever will be committed, including those sins which may be tormenting us today—so that in some dark recess of our hearts we may be thinking, "God can't possibly forgive me for that."

Should He? No. Did He? Yes, absolutely, unequivocally, and irrevocably. How? Through the sacrifice of His Son, Jesus Christ. As Isaiah wrote, "All we like sheep have gone astray; we have turned, every one, to his own way; and the LORD has laid on Him the iniquity of us all," Isaiah 53:6.

But does forgiveness mean that we are free to go on sinning? Far from it. Such thinking denies the blackness of sin, and even worse, the incalculable cost of salvation. Paul wrote, "I have been crucified with Christ; it is no longer I who live, but Christ lives in me; and the life which I now live in the flesh I live by faith in the Son of God, who loved me and gave Himself for me," Galatians 2:20.

It is at the cross of Jesus that sin appears at its blackest, and grace shines at its brightest. Indeed, through the power of the Holy Spirit, God has planted the Tree of Calvary in our hearts.

And it has become the Tree of Life.

# Viewer Discretion Advised

1 Corinthians10:1-13

*As certain as we should be of our salvation in Christ, we should never presume that we cannot throw away God's blessings.*

In 2013, the History Channel aired a miniseries titled *The Bible*. While I found the overall presentation disappointing, I was intrigued by the "Viewer Discretion Advised" warnings that appeared between program segments. Of course, I expected such advisories with some types of programming. For example, news footage showing the aftermath of terrorist attacks or deaths from a natural disaster. But a TV show about the Bible? C'mon.

But then I realized, if certain biblical events had been filmed in detail and aired unedited, the graphic images would warrant a viewer advisory, too. Consider the worldwide flood in which all humanity perished, with the exception of Noah and his immediate family. Or the destruction of Sodom and Gomorrah. Or the overthrow of Jericho, when all inhabitants of the city—male and female, young and old, even the livestock—were put to death.

Events like these would warrant the warning, "The following program contains graphic images which some viewers may find disturbing. Viewer discretion is advised." Only, not viewer discretion in the TV sense of "be warned before viewing," but in the biblical sense of "view and be warned."

When Paul wrote about the sad history of the Israelites, especially their indifferent sinning despite all of the Lord's goodness, he was in essence issuing a viewer discretion advisory. View and be warned. Their judgment was meant to warn us, as stated in 1 Corinthians 10:11, "Now all these things happened to them as examples, and they were written for *our* admonition, upon whom the ends of the ages have come."

What happened to the Israelites? They grew indifferent toward the Lord and His Word, and as a result, suffered the consequences. Paul wrote, "And do not become idolaters as were some of them. As it is written, 'The people sat down to eat and drink, and rose up to play.' Nor let us commit sexual immorality, as some of them did, and in one day twenty-three thousand fell; nor let us tempt Christ, as some of them also tempted, and were destroyed by serpents; nor complain, as some of them also complained, and were destroyed by the destroyer," 1 Corinthians 10:7-10.

Without question, the viewer discretionary warning in 1 Corinthians 10 is stark and sobering. Yet, it is a warning that Christians need to hear. For when God warns us against spiritual indifference and deliberate sinning, when He declares, "Viewer discretion is advised," it is only because He loves us. He wants us to possess the blessings that are ours in Christ, and never to throw them away in carelessness or indifference. He wants us to understand that sin is serious and salvation is serious. And when *we* are serious, we are no longer indifferent.

Yes, God wants us to be certain of our salvation in Christ. This is why He speaks of it so often in Scripture. "There is therefore now no condemnation to those who are in Christ Jesus," Romans 8:1. Or, "If you confess with your mouth the Lord Jesus and believe in your heart that God has raised Him from the dead, you will be saved," Romans 10:9.

Yet, as certain as we should be of our salvation, we should never presume that we cannot throw God's blessings away. We can, and what happened to ancient Israel is the proof. Paul wrote, "God is faithful," 1 Corinthians 10:13. His faithfulness to us is never in question. No, the question lies with our faithfulness to Him.

Several months ago, I ordered a magazine from Publishers Clearing House. And since that time, I've been barraged by daily emails about the PCH sweepstakes, emails with titles like "Mark, join the winners' circle" or, "Mark, we need to hear from you" or, "Mark, you have an elite communication from the PCH Prize Patrol." The most recent email was "Mark, avoid disqualification. Act now."

So, I took the email seriously. I acted. I read through yet another long, boring email advertising magazines I will never read and merchandise I will never buy; just so I could reach the final SUBMIT ENTRY button. I followed the directions and meticulously checked all the appropriate boxes, despite the knowledge that the odds of winning the PCH sweepstakes were 1 in 215,500,000, and that I was three times more likely to be struck by lightning.

If I am willing to be that meticulous to avoid disqualification for a prize I have almost no chance of winning, how meticulous should I be to avoid disqualification from the prize—eternal life, eternal salvation—that God has freely and undeservedly given me in Jesus Christ?

Paul wrote in 1 Corinthians 9:26-27, "Therefore I run thus: not with uncertainty. Thus I fight: not as one who beats the air. But I discipline my body and bring it into subjection, lest, when I have preached to others, I myself should become disqualified."

# When Facing Adversity

James 5:7-11

*When facing adversity, how are we to respond? Are we to patiently overcome or anemically surrender? Are we to rejoice or retaliate?*

**Be Patient**

In this section of Scripture James uses two Greek words to describe patience. The first of these is *MACROTHEMEO*, which means long-suffering or long-tempered. The second Greek word is *HUPOMONE*, literally meaning "to remain under," that is, having the ability to remain under difficult circumstances and heavy burdens without giving up or giving in.

Where does such patience originate? From the certain knowledge that God will act on our behalf at the right time and in the right way. To illustrate, James uses the example of a farmer. "Therefore be patient, brethren, until the coming of the Lord. See how the farmer waits for the precious fruit of the earth, waiting patiently for it until it receives the early and latter rain," James 5:7. The farmer can be patient because he knows that eventually, inevitably, the rains will fall, the drought will end, the crops will grow, and the harvest will come.

When facing adversity, we, too, can be patient because we know that eventually, inevitably, God will deliver us. This is not a tired cliché like "tough times never last but tough people do." This is a glorious reality because it is based on Scriptural fact. Peter wrote in his First Epistle, "But may the God of all grace, who called us to His eternal glory by Christ Jesus, after you have suffered a while, perfect, establish, strengthen, and settle you," 1 Peter 5:10.

Whatever the adversity, has God ever failed you in the past? And if He hasn't failed you in the past, will He fail you in the future? And if God doesn't always give you exactly what you want, doesn't He always give you exactly what you need?

## Be Steadfast

James wrote, "You also be patient. Establish your hearts, for the coming of the Lord is at hand," James 5:8. The Greek word for "establish" in this verse means to "make strong, firm, immovable." But what makes us strong and steadfast when facing adversity? Money? Possessions? Connections? Relationships? Philosophy? These are merely props, not solid foundations. If you're facing adversity, the stamina and stability you need is waiting in the Word of God.

Jesus once told a parable about wise and foolish builders. One builder built his house on bedrock; the other built his house on sand. When rains fell and floods came and winds blew and beat on both houses, only one house remained standing—not because of its builder, but because of its bedrock, the Word of God. "Therefore," said Jesus, "whoever hears these sayings of Mine, and does them, I will liken him to a wise man who built his house on the rock," Matthew 7:24.

## Be Kind

In the original Greek, James 5:9 is literally, "Don't go on grumbling against each other, brothers." Don't go on, because grumbling is what the first readers of James were already doing. They were taking their frustrations out on one another, their families and friends. Haven't we all done the same when facing adversity?

However, adversity should not tear us apart. It should bring us together. And this is especially true of Christians— people who know from Scripture that each of us is sinful, each of us is saved by grace, and each of us is forgiven in the precious blood of Jesus Christ. What justification, then, can we have for criticizing, grumbling, and rolling our eyes at one another? What if God grumbled about us?

I don't know of any Bible passages that tell Christians to like each other. But I can cite many Bible passages that call upon Christians to love each other; to love with that same great, committed, self-sacrificing, and undeserved love with which Jesus Christ has loved each of us.

### Be Certain of God's Very Best

When facing adversity, do you expect the best from God or the worst? To set our expectations, James reminds us of the Old Testament believer Job. Remember him? If you think your life is riddled with problems, take a close look at his.

Within the space of hours, Job lost his health, wealth, possessions, servants, livelihood, and all ten of his children. Imagine burying ten children in a single day. Given such adversities, we can understand Job saying, "Why did I not die at birth? Why did I not perish when I came from the womb?" Job 3:11. Translation: "I wish I had never been born."

But when circumstances were at their worst, Job received the very best from God. As James reminds us, "Indeed, we count them blessed who endure. You have heard of the perseverance of Job and seen the end intended by the Lord— that the Lord is very compassionate and merciful," James 5:11.

And what did the Lord bring about for Job? After all the pain, loss, and heartache, this is what Job received from God: "Now the LORD blessed the latter days of Job more than his beginning," Job 42:12.

Are you facing adversity today? Is your life a mess? Has everything gone wrong? Are you hurting? Are you expecting the very worst from God? Stop. Why expect the worst from God, when He has already given you the best He has to give in His Son, Jesus Christ? As Paul wrote in Romans 8:32, "He who did not spare His own Son, but delivered Him up for us all, how shall He not with Him also freely give us all things?"

# When God Delays

John 11:17-27, 38-45

*At times, we all go through desperate circumstances in which our hopes, like Lazarus, grow ill, die, and are laid to rest.*

When Lazarus became ill, his sisters Mary and Martha sent an urgent note to Jesus, saying, "Lord, behold, he whom You love is sick," John 11:3. Yet, instead of going immediately to Lazarus, Jesus delayed for two days. During this delay, Lazarus died.

At the funeral, both Mary and Martha spoke identical words to Jesus, "Lord, if You had been here, my brother would not have died," John 11:21, 32. Their lament contained grief, disappointment, and perhaps even a hint of reproach. To paraphrase, "Lord, if You had been here on time; if You had acted instead of delayed, this tragedy would never have happened."

Have we not all spoken similar words to God when our prayers go unanswered and our problems go unsolved? Of course. Yet, before we accuse God of capriciousness or tardiness, let's consider His reasons for delaying.

## God Loves Us

When God delays, He does so out of love. This may be difficult to understand and even more difficult to accept, especially in times of trouble, but it is nevertheless true. According to John 11:5-6, "Now Jesus loved Martha and her sister and Lazarus. So, when He heard that he was sick, He stayed two more days in the place where He was." Notice the "so." Jesus delayed going to Bethany because of His love for Mary, Martha, and Lazarus.

The word for love in these verses is *AGAPE*; that love of deep understanding and unswerving commitment, and the same word used in the familiar verse, "For God so loved the world that He gave His only begotten Son," John 3:16. We may not always understand the circumstances. We may not see the beauty of the complete picture until the entire puzzle is pieced together. However, we can always be certain that God's delays are the result of His great love for us. And this is what enables us to hold on and press forward. As the hymnist wrote, "One day I shall see clearly, that He hath loved me dearly."

### God Is Preparing a Glorious Solution

Jesus told Martha, "Did I not say to you that if you would believe you would see the glory of God?" John 11:40. I suggest that God says the same to us every day, amid every problem. "Trust Me. Wait for Me to act. You will see My glory."

As much as I have wrestled with problems in my life, I can truthfully say that Almighty God has never failed to force even the worst circumstances to serve my best interests. Mary and Martha wanted Lazarus to be healed. The Lord gave them a resurrection. Which solution was more glorious?

God may be delaying in your life, but remember His promise: "Call upon Me in the day of trouble; I will deliver you, and you shall glorify Me," Psalm 50:15. "I *will*," said God. Not if. Not maybe. Rather, the certainty of deliverance and the inevitability of glory.

### God Is Strengthening Faith

I can imagine Mary and Martha standing at the bedside of dying Lazarus; dabbing his feverish forehead with cool, wet cloths; whispering encouragement: "Don't worry, brother. Jesus is on the way. When He arrives, everything will be fine."

Yet, away from the deathbed of Lazarus, perhaps the sisters were constantly peering out the window, scanning the horizon for any sign of Christ's coming, and asking each other in hushed voices, "Where is He? What is taking Jesus so long?"

We understand Mary and Martha because we are like them. Yet, too often we forget that when God delays, He is allowing something mighty, wondrous, and holy to happen. He is allowing time for the wrong type of hope to die and be buried—like Lazarus, and for His Spirit to strengthen our faith and focus our hope on Jesus Christ.

## God Is Directing Us to His Life-Giving Word

"Why is God's Word so important?" I've heard many people ask this question. In answering, I won't direct you to the Third Commandment ("Remember the Sabbath day, to keep it holy," Exodus 20:8), as important as it is.

Instead, I will direct you to a cemetery outside of Bethany, where Jesus Christ stood before the sepulcher of dead, decaying Lazarus, and with a loud voice cried out, "Lazarus, come forth!" And at the power of God's word, Lazarus came forth, bound by grave clothes but no longer bound by the grave.

Friends, if you and I need more incentive to hear God's word, I can't imagine what it would be.

Knowing why God at times delays enables us to proclaim with the psalmist, "I wait for the LORD, my soul waits, and in His word I do hope," Psalm 130:5.

# When God Disciplines

Hebrews 12:5-13

*Why does God discipline us? Is His intent to harm or heal, to instruct or destruct?*

When I was a boy, no phrase worried me more than "You just wait until your father gets home." Wait I did, peeking out the window while contemplating my fate. And when dad's car finally pulled into the driveway, I scrambled for my room, closed the door, sat down on the bed like a saintly cherub, hoping that dad would be too tired or too busy to discipline. He never was. Whether a scolding or spanking, I got what I deserved and it hurt. But all these years later, I understand how that discipline helped shape me into the person I am.

Should we expect anything less from our perfect Father in heaven? No. When He disciplines, He does so in absolute love and with great purpose; namely, to strengthen, train, and instruct us, so that we can run our Christian race with great stamina and perseverance. To quote the writer of Hebrews, "Now no chastening seems to be joyful for the present, but painful; nevertheless, afterward it yields the peaceable fruit of righteousness to those who have been trained by it," Hebrews 12:11.

**Good Things from Bad Things**

Let's admit it. When bad things happen in life, we're tempted to blame God. This is nothing new. Adam said, "God, it's the woman *You* gave me." Eve said, "God, it's the serpent *You* made." Yet, in reality, we bring many bad things upon ourselves through our own bad habits, bad choices, and bad behaviors.

The holy God is never the source of evil. As James explained, "Let no one say when he is tempted, 'I am tempted by God'; for God cannot be tempted by evil, nor does He Himself tempt anyone," James 1:13. Yet, one of the great promises of Scripture is that God will force even the bad things that befall us to serve our best interests. This is what Paul meant when he wrote, "And we know that all things work together for good to those who love God, to those who are the called according to His purpose," Romans 8:28.

As a child of God, you can be certain of this: Whatever difficulties you may be facing in life, somehow, somewhere, some way, at some time, God will make even the "bad things" serve your good. Knowing this, isn't the burden lighter? Isn't running the Christian race easier?

## Child Training

Decades ago, the principal of the Christian school I attended kept a paddle on display in his classroom. And when circumstances warranted, he used it. Back then, if we were paddled at school, we were usually paddled also at home. Imagine that in today's over-dramatized, over-victimized society.

Yet, the paddle was but one small part of the classroom. In the same room we learned reading, writing, and arithmetic; how to study, interact, and obey the rules. The overall goal of the school was to develop well-rounded Christian individuals. And when God disciplines, His goal is the same.

The Greek word for *discipline* occurs eight times in Hebrews 12:5-13—five times as a noun, three times as a verb. The nouns and verbs look similar because they share the same root: *PAIS. PAIS* means child. Above all else, when God disciplines, He is child-training; that is, training His own dear children. His Fatherly intent is to help, not hurt; instruct, not destruct; thereby transforming us into well-rounded, mature Christian individuals, who can run the race of faith with perseverance and bear witness to the grace of God in Jesus Christ.

When we encounter problems in life—an illness, loss,

difficult relationship—instead of accusing God of negligence, perhaps we should ask Him, "God, what is this problem meant to teach me?" Through need He may be teaching us to rely on Him. Through silence He may be teaching us to talk more with Him. Through weakness He may be teaching us the all-important lesson of Grace Alone, the very same lesson that Paul learned when God disciplined him, saying, "My grace is sufficient for you, for My strength is made perfect in weakness," 2 Corinthians 12:9.

## Absolute Love

As parents, we sometimes convince ourselves that love means giving our children whatever they want. But this is not true love. True love means giving our children what they need, saying "yes" to some requests and "no" to others. True love means disciplining, not appeasing; instilling values, not worldly instincts.

Some would call this "tough love." However, the Bible would call it *AGAPE* love. *AGAPE*, the Greek word which denotes the highest form of love, which is also God's love. A love that transcends the deepest emotion to embrace the deepest commitment. A love that is unshakably focused on true need instead of mere want. The type of love that moved Jesus to embrace even the cross to save us.

When God disciplines, He does so in the same love in which He redeemed us. I know it's hard to say, harder to accept, and hardest of all to share with a person facing problems and pain; nevertheless, the biblical truth is that when God disciplines, He is loving us. Am I struggling with illness? It's because God loves me. Am I dealing with loss? It's because God loves me. Have I not yet won the lottery? It's because God loves me.

## Thanks, Dad

I have vivid memories of sitting on the living room sofa, with my dad hovering over me to ensure I was memorizing the questions, answers, and Bible passages in Martin Luther's Small Catechism. "Dad," I would moan, "this isn't fair. All the other kids are outside playing. I'm stuck inside learning this Bible stuff." And my dad would answer, "Mark, the other kids aren't my responsibility. You're my son."

Every time I go through difficulties and am able to keep moving forward in faith because of all that "Bible stuff," I think about sitting on that living room sofa. And I thank God for my father, a father who cared enough to discipline me.

When God disciplines us, He is treating us as His children and His responsibility. Shouldn't this fill us with delight, joy, and confidence? Obstacles will come in the Christian race of faith. But when they do come, remember this word of encouragement from God Himself, "My son, do not despise the chastening of the LORD, nor be discouraged when you are rebuked by Him; for whom the LORD loves He chastens, and scourges every son whom He receives," Hebrews 12:5-6.

# When Prayers Go Unanswered

Luke 11:1-13

*You've heard the saying, "God answers every prayer, but sometimes the answer is no." Yet, isn't hearing "no" better than hearing nothing?*

What should we do when our prayers go unanswered? Should we give up? Should we accuse God of indifference, or worse, of breaking His promise to answer our prayers? Or, should we ask ourselves what the silence of God may be teaching us?

**Talking or Instructing**

For many people, prayer is like a soda machine. They only visit the machine when hot and thirsty. They drop in a few coins, that is, say a few words. They make a personal selection: Coke, Pepsi, Fanta; health, money, marriage. And so long as the machine delivers the right product at the right time, they are happy. But let the machine deliver a different product or nothing at all, they bang on the coin return with both fists and storm off.

Of course, prayer is not a soda machine. And when it is treated like one—like a coin transaction in which we get what we deserve instead of getting the undeserved, why would God answer such a prayer? Would you?

If prayers go unanswered, perhaps the reason lies in the manner in which we are praying. Are we talking with God or instructing Him? Are we approaching God like a heavenly Father or like a soda machine?

**Right Motives or Wrong Motives**

An elderly man found a magic lamp on the beach.

Delighted, he rubbed the lamp vigorously until a genie appeared. "Because you have released me," said the genie, "I will grant you one wish." The man thought for a while, then replied, "My brother and I had a terrible argument thirty years ago, and he hasn't spoken to me since. I wish for his forgiveness."

The genie granted the request, but then added, "I'm puzzled. Most people wish for fame, fortune, or power. But you asked for your brother's forgiveness. Why? Is it because you are elderly, sick, and dying?" "No," said the man. "My brother is the one who is old, sick, and dying. And he's worth about sixty million dollars."

The apostle James wrote, "You ask and do not receive, because you ask amiss, that you may spend it on your pleasures," James 4:3. Are we praying for something out of selflessness or selfishness, with the right motives or the wrong ones, in conformity with God's will or our own will?

## Humility or Pride

Do you remember the *Parable of the Pharisee and Publican*, Luke 18:9-14, the story of two men who went into the temple to pray? The Pharisee stood in the spotlight of his own righteousness and prayed, "God, I thank You that I am not like other men—extortioners, unjust, adulterers, or even as this tax collector. I fast twice a week; I give tithes of all that I possess," Luke 18:11-12.

By contrast, the tax collector stood at a distance, in the shadows. So great was his shame, guilt, and consciousness of sin that he "would not so much as raise his eyes to heaven, but beat his breast, saying, 'God, be merciful to me a sinner,' " Luke 18:13. According to Jesus, the humble, contrite tax collector went home justified, with his prayers heard and answered. The prayers of the prideful Pharisee, however, were not heeded, because he was not praying to God, but praying to himself.

## Helpful or Harmful

When my sons were small, I gave them a variety of gifts: Legos, video consoles and games, bicycles, popsicles, clothes, books, sports equipment—over time, probably half the inventory at TOYS R US. Yes, I made mistakes. But as a father who loved his sons and wanted only the best for them, I always tried to give good gifts and avoid harmful ones. I never substituted dynamite for firecrackers. I never exchanged milk of magnesia for milk from a cow. Nor would you.

Jesus said, "If you then, being evil, know how to give good gifts to your children, how much more will your Father who is in heaven give good things to those who ask Him!" Matthew 7:11. God is committed to our eternal welfare and eternal salvation. No matter how much we plead, He will never give us anything that may prove detrimental to our faith. And for this we should praise Him instead of accusing Him of sleepy indifference or heartless capriciousness.

## Giving Up or Pressing On

Do you recall the account of the Canaanite woman in Matthew 15:21-28, how she came to Jesus for help, and how Jesus responded? At first, He did not answer her a word. Then He walked away. Then He told the woman that He had come to help Israelites, not Canaanites. Then He said, "It is not good to take the children's bread and throw it to the little dogs." Undeterred, the woman replied, "Yes, Lord, yet even the little dogs eat the crumbs which fall from their masters' table."

Why did Jesus walk away from the woman? Because He wanted her to follow Him. Why was Jesus silent? Because He wanted the woman to speak to Him. Why did Jesus set up so many obstacles before answering her prayer? Because He wanted the woman's faith to be a great faith. And when our prayers go unanswered, when God seems to be silent or walk away or rebuff our petitions—He only wants the same for us.

He wants our faith to be a great faith.

# Wrestling with God

Genesis 32:22-30

*We may not have wrestled with God by the banks of the Jabbok river, but we have all wrestled with God through long nights of prayer.*

Late that night, Jacob stood on the bank of the Jabbok River—frightened, worried, sleepless. Those dearest to him, his wives Leah and Rachel and his children, had already crossed the Jabbok. Jacob was now alone. Somewhere in the darkness, his vengeful brother Esau approached with four hundred men. Would Esau kill Jacob? Would he enslave Jacob's wives and children?

On that dismal night, Jacob must have stood, sat, paced, fretted, and most of all wondered, "Where is God?" Surely, God would deliver him; for God had set him on this journey, saying, "Return to the land of your fathers and to your family, and I will be with you," Genesis 31:3.

Did God help Jacob that night? Yes, but in a way Jacob could not have anticipated. God wrestled with Jacob. The Hebrew word translated as "wrestled" literally means to pound down, make small, and get dusty. Imagine two opponents grappling and rolling in the dust. This is what God and Jacob were doing.

Even more astonishing, God was the one to initiate the wrestling, the first to crouch in a wrestling stance. "Then Jacob was left alone; and a Man wrestled *with him* until the breaking of day," Genesis 32:24. And that this Man was God is evident from Jacob's own words, "For I have seen God face to face, and my life is preserved," Genesis 32:30.

Does God wrestle with us? Yes. We may not wrestle with Him by the banks of the Jabbok River, but we do wrestle with God through long, sleepless nights of prayer. Our wrestling with God may not raise dust, but it often raises questions: "God, why are You opposing me? Why are You hurting me and pinning me down?"

## A Personal Match

Wrestling is a personal combat: hand to hand, face to face, one to one. We may not view God's wrestling with us as personal attention, but it is. He comes to us where we are, as with Jacob at the Jabbok—as we lie sleepless in bed or wait for the results of a medical test or struggle with finances—and gives us what we need, including a personalized wrestling match. At times, we need to wrestle with God, and He knows those times. At times, He needs to pin us down to lift us up, and tenderly hurt us in order to heal us.

## Down for the Count

As a boy, I loved to wrestle with my dad. Amazingly, I won almost every match, pinning dad's shoulders to the mat for a count of ONE-TWO-THREE; and afterwards strutting around the living room, arms raised in victory.

But sometimes, especially when I strutted too much, Dad pinned me down for the count; holding me firmly despite my giggling, squirming, and eventual complaining. Why? To keep me grounded in reality. To remind me who was in charge. To show me my limitations. To teach me that there were some things I could not do on my own.

Jacob learned this lesson by wrestling with God. You and I need to learn it, too. For there is no greater comfort than knowing God is in charge. "God, You are in charge of my life, my problems, my finances, and my illnesses." In biblical terms, when we surrender to God, we always win the match.

## Living in Power

Wrestling with God not only reveals our weaknesses, it also displays God's strength. Jacob also learned this lesson at the Jabbok River. One touch from God dislocated Jacob's hip.

To oppose such power would be foolish and destructive. By contrast, to rely on that almighty power of God is to undertake every God-pleasing endeavor with absolute confidence, whether crossing the Jabbok River or repairing a troubled marriage.

## Faith is Victory

Here is a strange verse: "Now when He saw that He did not prevail against him," Genesis 32:25. How could God not overpower Jacob—a mortal man with a sinful nature and a résumé of personal schemes and personal failures; a man who was so afraid of his brother Esau that, when he finally encountered Esau, he bowed to the ground seven times?

Was it truly that God could not defeat Jacob? No. Rather, through that long night of wrestling, God taught Jacob that victory comes through faith.

An overcoming faith is exactly what God wanted Jacob to have, a faith which declares, "No matter how bad things are, God, I know Who You are. I know what You've done for me in the past and will do for me in the future. Therefore, I will not let You go unless You bless me."

Through wrestling with God, Jacob learned that God's intent all along, through the bumps, scrapes, submission holds, and raised dust, was to let Jacob win the match.

## Better Wrestlers

None of us enjoy wrestling with God. The wrestling can hurt. Yet, each time we do wrestle with the Almighty; each time He calls us out, sizes us up, crouches into His wrestling stance, seems to push us away or pin us down; we become better wrestlers. Better by realizing how personally involved God is in our lives. Better by remembering that He is in control. Better by relying on His strength. Better by knowing that in the end, no matter how long the match or fierce the bout, God is going to let us win.

# Seven Letters

# To Ephesus

Revelation 2:1-7

*"Nevertheless I have this against you, that you have left your first love."*

The letter of Revelation was first addressed to seven churches in Asia Minor: Ephesus, Smyrna, Pergamos, Thyatira, Sardis, Philadelphia, and Laodicea. All seven of these churches were connected by a circuitous road, and were listed in Revelation in the exact order they would be reached if traveling north from Ephesus.

Though the letter of Revelation was first addressed to these seven churches, Jesus also intended it for the "mailbox" of every Christian congregation. This is clear from the reference to Christ's "servants" in Revelation 1:1, and also from Revelation 1:3, where blessing is promised to everyone who reads and believes the message of this prophetic letter.

Each of the seven letters to the seven churches has a similar format: the name of the city, followed by some aspect of the vision of Christ given in Revelation 1:12-18 and meant to address particular circumstances in that church, followed by an evaluation of the church and corrective action if needed, followed by the familiar call to action: "He who has an ear, let him hear what the Spirit says to the churches."

## The City of Ephesus

Even in antiquity, Ephesus was known as the "light of Asia." The city was so important that every Roman proconsul appointed to the governorship of Asia was required *by law* to enter the province at Ephesus.

Ephesus was the financial center of Asia. Located near the mouth of the Cayster River and at the juncture of several trade routes, and with a spacious harbor on the Aegean Sea, Ephesus thrived with commerce. Its main road, the Arcadian Way, was one hundred feet wide, paved with marble, and lined with rows of columns.

At the time Revelation was written, Ephesus had a population of nearly 300,000. The city was also a cultural and religious center, featuring numerous statues, shrines, fountains, communal baths, public toilets, and various government buildings. It also had an Odeon or concert hall; a 25,000-seat amphitheater—the very theater where a mob rioted against Paul and his gospel, as recorded in Acts 19; also the renowned Library of Celsus, with its twelve thousand scrolls or books; a brothel connected to the library by a tunnel; and the world-famous temple of the fertility goddess Artemis—one of the seven wonders of the ancient world.

Emperor worship was also prevalent in Ephesus, as elsewhere in Asia Minor. One of the ancient inscriptions still visible on the Library of Celsus reads, "From the Emperor Caesar August, the son of the god, the greatest of the priests."

**The Congregation in Ephesus**

Paul founded the Ephesian congregation on his second missionary journey. His initial visit was brief. However, when he returned to Ephesus on his third missionary journey, he spent nearly three years with the Ephesian Christians—longer than with any other congregation.

Over time, the Ephesian congregation was served by many New Testament notables: the apostle Paul, the great orator Apollos, husband and wife missionaries Aquilla and Priscilla, and young pastor Timothy. According to early church writings, the apostle John, the writer of Revelation, also served the congregation at Ephesus. Visit Ephesus today, and you'll see the alleged tomb of John.

**The Message to Ephesus**

After identifying Himself as personally and intimately involved in the ministry of the Ephesian congregation, upholding its ministers and walking lovingly in its midst, Jesus tells the congregation, "I know your works, your labor, your patience, and that you cannot bear those who are evil. And you have tested those who say they are apostles and are not, and have found them liars; and you have persevered and have patience, and have labored for My name's sake and have not become weary," Revelation 2:2-3.

In many respects, the Ephesian congregation was a model congregation. Hard work. Endurance. Commitment. Thirty to forty years earlier, as recorded in Acts 20, Paul had solemnly warned the Ephesian elders about false teachers from within and without. They had heeded this warning, as we know from Christ's own words in Revelation 2:2, "And you have tested those who say they are apostles and are not, and have found them liars."

And yet, despite all the hard work and perseverance and doctrinal integrity, something was seriously wrong within the Ephesian congregation. Jesus described the problem in Revelation 2:4, saying, "Nevertheless I have this against you, that you have left your first love."

What is meant by "first love"? Had the Ephesian Christians forsaken their first-love for God? No. Lukewarm love for God was the problem in the Laodicean congregation. Had the Ephesian Christians forsaken their love of the truth? Again, no. They were testing apostolic claims in order to separate truth from falsehood. Then, what type of first-love had the congregation in Ephesus forsaken? In all likelihood, they had lost meaningful, active love for one another.

Jesus taught His disciples the importance of loving one another when He said in John 13:34-35, "A new commandment I give to you, that you love one another; as I have loved you, that you also love one another. By this all will know that you are My disciples, if you have love for one another." It is the love Christians have for God and for each other that shines so brightly in this dark world of hatred and vengeance—shines like the "seven golden lampstands" mentioned in Revelation.

Here is the staggering reality: While the Christians in Ephesus had a love for the truth, they had lost a Christ-like love for one another. They were doctrinally pure but lovingly poor. So serious is this love-loss in the eyes of Jesus Christ that He warns the Ephesians, "Remember therefore from where you have fallen; repent and do the first works, or else I will come to you quickly and remove your lampstand from its place—unless you repent," Revelation 2:5.

Doctrinal purity is vitally important. Yet, doctrinal purity without brotherly love is unacceptable to God, is the "sounding brass" and "clanging cymbal" of 1 Corinthians 13, noise without melody, action without substance. The church at Ephesus was an orthodox church. But Jesus told its members that He would rather have no church at all in Ephesus than to have a confessional church with no brotherly love. A staggering, humbling thought.

"You have left your first love," said Jesus. But He also told the Ephesians how to get that first-love back, saying, "Remember therefore from where you have fallen; repent and do the first works," Revelation 2:5. Think of His advice as the three R's.

REMEMBER: Remember the way things were when your congregation was filled with this type of first-love.

REPENT: Change the way you're doing things. Love as Christ has loved you. This type of love—the Greek word used is *AGAPE*—is a love of determined action, not emotional feeling. Even when you don't *feel* that brotherly or sisterly love, even when you have no real reason to love, go on loving each other anyway. This is the way God loves you, isn't it?

And finally, RESUME: "Do the first works," said Jesus. This is not only the secret of a strong romance. This is the secret to a strong Christian congregation.

"He who has an ear, let him hear what the Spirit says to the churches."

# To Smyrna

Revelation 2:8-11

*"Do not fear any of those things which you are about to suffer."*

From Ephesus we travel thirty-five miles north to the church in Smyrna, often called the "suffering church" because of the hardships it endured for the sake of Christ.

**The City of Smyrna**

In antiquity Smyrna was known as the "Glory of Asia." It was a prosperous city, ideally located for commerce. Its harbor was deeper and better sheltered than the one in Ephesus, and could be completely closed in times of war.

Smyrna was also situated on the only trade route for the Hermus River Valley. All goods from this valley passed into Smyrna's marketplace and out of its harbor. Over time the city became a major importer and exporter, especially valued for its fine wine and myrrh. In fact, the name *Smyrna* means myrrh; one of the spices presented to Jesus by the Wise Men, and later used to anoint the body of Jesus for burial. As Smyrna grew prosperous, it grew populous. At the time Revelation was written, the city had a population of nearly 150,000.

And Smyrna was a beautiful city, too. Beautiful harbor. Beautiful buildings. Beautiful weather thanks to the gentle westerly wind known as the *Zephyr*. A beautiful hill, which residents called the "Crown of Smyrna," overlooking the city. And beautiful streets like the Golden Street, which traversed the city from harbor to foothills, and was lined with magnificent temples dedicated to pagan gods.

Smyrna also boasted a famous stadium, library, and the largest theater in Asia Minor. It also claimed to be the birthplace of the Greek poet Homer. It was a proud city, proud enough for the historian Theodor Mommsen to describe it as a "paradise of municipal vanity."

## The Congregation in Smyrna

Scripture does not provide the history of the church in Smyrna. It may have been founded by Paul, or members of the Ephesian congregation, or even by converts returning from the First Pentecost in Jerusalem. We simply don't know.

We do know, however, based on other Christian churches of that era, that the congregation at Smyrna was likely small in size and that it met in humble surroundings—this in stark contrast to the pagan temples adorning the city—and that it was primarily composed of the poor and uneducated, and perhaps even some slaves.

According to the letter from Jesus to Smyrna, this small, unpretentious congregation was suffering. Indeed, notice the language in this letter: "tribulation, poverty, blasphemy, prison, tested, death."

Despite its beauty and prosperity, Smyrna was a dangerous place for Christians. The city was extremely devoted to Rome, both in its political affiliation and in its worship of the Roman emperor. Smyrna was the first city in the ancient world to build a temple for *Dea Roma*, the patron goddess of Rome. In A.D. 26, Smyrna outbid six other cities for the right to build a temple for the worship of Emperor Tiberius; a capable leader, but best known for his treason trials, murders, and sexual perversions.

Once a year, residents of Asia Minor were required by law to appear before a Roman magistrate, burn a "pinch of incense" at the altar of Caesar, and proclaim that Caesar was *Dominus et Deus*, that is, Lord and God. Failure to do so was viewed as treason and was punishable by death. At the least, those who refused to worship Caesar were scorned, ostracized, persecuted, and prevented from holding jobs. Significantly, the word for "poverty" in Revelation 2:9 does not mean having financial trouble; it means having nothing at all—the type of poverty that resulted when poor Christians were refused jobs simply because they were Christians, because they called Jesus Christ *Dominus et Deus* instead of the Roman emperor.

But there was another reason for Christian suffering in Smyrna. Jesus alluded to it in Revelation 2:9, saying, "I know the blasphemy of those who say they are Jews and are not, but are a synagogue of Satan." Smyrna was home to a large number of Jews, and some of these Jews were slandering Christians in the hope of disassociating themselves from Christianity and causing trouble for believers in Christ.

### The Message to Smyrna

What comfort did Jesus offer the hurting Christians in Smyrna? How do His words comfort us when we face suffering?

First, Jesus identified Himself as "the First and the Last, who was dead, and came to life," Revelation 2:8. What are these words, if not a precious summary of Christ's work of redemption, His death for our sins, His resurrection for our justification? As Paul wrote in Romans 4:25, Christ "was delivered up because of our offenses, and was raised because of our justification."

From the very first line of His letter to the suffering Christians in Smyrna, Jesus reminded them, "I am your eternally faithful God. I have infinite power and infinite love. I love you so much that I died for your sins. My resurrection is the guarantee of your resurrection." Is there a better description of God for those who are suffering or about to suffer?

Translate this into our own era and our own increasingly chaotic, dangerous world. Nuclear ambitions in North Korea. Chemical weapons in Syria. Increasing hostility toward Christians, even in the United States. Islamic terrorists demanding of Christians—a demand no different in essence from the one in Smyrna: "Worship Allah or die."

Yet, is any nation too strong for the Lord? Is any sickness too strong for the Lord? Is any corrupt politician or troubled marriage or heartless dictator or design of Satan too strong for the Lord? Of course not. And this is what Jesus was telling the suffering Christians in Smyrna when He called Himself "the First and the Last, who was dead, and came to life."

However, when we suffer, it is important to remember not only God's infinite power and redemptive love. It is equally important to remember His awareness, understanding, and personal involvement in our suffering. Jesus addressed this very matter in Revelation 2:9, saying, "I *know* your works, tribulation, and poverty . . . ; I *know* the blasphemy of those who say they are Jews and are not, but are a synagogue of Satan."

Jesus not only said "I know," He also pictured it when He pictured Himself walking in the very middle of every Christian congregation. And Jesus proved it when He shared in our humanity; carried our sins, sicknesses, and sorrows; and suffered in our place. And so the Bible states, "For we do not have a High Priest who cannot sympathize with our weaknesses, but was in all points tempted as we are, yet without sin. Let us therefore come boldly to the throne of grace, that we may obtain mercy and find grace to help in time of need," Hebrews 4:15-16.

If you are suffering, consider the comfort Jesus provided in His letter to Smyrna. He is your almighty God. He is always present and always loving. He understands your suffering, and your suffering is under His control. He is faithful to you, and calls you to faithful, patient endurance with this glorious promise, "Be faithful until death, and I will give you the crown of life," Revelation 2:10.

"He who has an ear, let him hear what the Spirit says to the churches."

# To Pergamos

Revelation 2:12-17

*"But I have a few things against you, because you have there those who hold the doctrine of Balaam."*

From Smyrna we travel fifteen miles northeast to the church in Pergamos, a church in danger of compromise.

## The City of Pergamos

Pergamos was located in the Caicus River Valley. As an inland city, it had no harbor and was not known for trade. But what Pergamos lacked in commerce, it gained in other important ways. Had there been a Chamber of Commerce in ancient Pergamos, it would have promoted the city as THE CAPITAL OF ASIA and THE FINEST MEDICAL CARE ANYWHERE and OUR WORLD-FAMOUS LIBRARY and THE BIRTHPLACE OF THE PHYSICIAN GALEN.

Had there been a "local churches" sign posted at the city limits of Pergamos, it would have read, *Temple of Asclepius*, *Temple of Serapis*, *Temple of Zeus*, *Temple of Athena*, and *Temple of Caesar Augustus*. There would have been no mention of the small Christian congregation meeting in private homes.

Pergamos was built at the bottom and at the top of a high hill. The upper city, known as the acropolis, contained many shrines and temples, that world-famous library, and one of the steepest amphitheaters in Asia Minor. The road which led from lower to upper Pergamos was appropriately named "The Sacred Way."

The library in Pergamos *was* world-famous. At a time in history when all books were written and copied by hand, this library contained more than 200,000 volumes. Only the library in Alexandria, Egypt was larger. This led to an intense rivalry between these two libraries.

And Pergamos *did* offer the best medical care available. The Asclepion, named for Asclepius, the god of healing, was located in lower Pergamos. While this temple was used for worship, it also served as a hospital; the ancient version of the Mayo Clinic. People from all over the world came to this medical center for healing.

The symbol of the god Asclepius was a serpent. His temple-hospital contained many non-poisonous snakes. The snakes crawled about freely. In the darkness of night, every patient hoped to be touched by a snake. The touch of a snake was believed to be the touch of the god Asclepius himself and to bring healing. To this very day, the serpent of Asclepius is used on the emblem of the American Medical Association.

## The Church in Pergamos

Nothing is known about the founding of the congregation in Pergamos. As was true in Smyrna, the church in Pergamos may have been started by Paul, or by members from other nearby Christian churches, or even by converts returning to Asia Minor after the First Pentecost.

## The Message to Pergamos

To a church in danger of compromise, Jesus described Himself as "He who has the sharp two-edged sword," Revelation 2:12. Similar imagery is used in 2:16, "the sword of My mouth," and again in 19:15, "Now out of His mouth goes a sharp sword."

One need not be a Christian of the First Century A.D. to understand this powerful symbolism. A sword is a sharp, lethal weapon meant to protect and destroy. A sword cuts through opposition. A doubled-edged sword can be swung in any direction. Most importantly, this double-edged sword is from the mouth of Christ, the Son of God, and therefore wields the power of God. This sword is the Word of God against which all foes, arguments and false teaching cannot stand.

The author of Hebrews wrote, "For the word of God is living and powerful, and sharper than any two-edged sword, piercing even to the division of soul and spirit, and of joints and marrow, and is a discerner of the thoughts and intents of the heart," Hebrews 4:12.

"I know your works, and where you dwell, where Satan's throne is," Revelation 2:13. I know. Those two precious words of awareness, sympathy, and personal involvement that Jesus spoke to all seven congregations in Asia Minor; words He still speaks to us today.

In what way was Pergamos the "throne" of Satan? First, Pergamos was the capital of Asia Minor, and as such, a seat of power for the pagan Roman government. Would we not call an empire that worshiped a pantheon of false gods, that committed the most heinous acts, and that murdered Christians for their faith, a throne of Satan?

Second, Pergamos was also a center of worship for Asclepius, the god of healing. The official title of this god was *Asclepius Soter*, literally, "Asclepius Savior." Christians know but one Savior, Jesus Christ. Would we not call giving Christ's title to a false god satanic? And what was the symbol of Asclepius? A serpent—the very form Satan took when he first slithered into human history.

Third, Pergamos housed the Altar of Zeus. During an excavation of Pergamos in the 1930s, this altar was moved stone by stone to Berlin, then refurbished and reconstructed. What does this altar resemble? A seat with armrests. A throne.

The Christian church in Pergamos may have gone unnoticed by most residents, but Satan took notice of the church and its gospel message and tried to eliminate both. His first ploy was persecution. And when that failed, Satan next turned to compromise. Throughout history, Satan has always been more effective attacking the Christian Church from within than from without.

This was happening in Pergamos. Some members of the congregation were saying, "It's perfectly fine to compromise

Scripture for a good cause. God won't mind. To reach the worldly, we must become worldly. To preach the true God, we must accept the traditional gods of Pergamos."

Compromising morals and truth is very evident in our nation today, and equally evident within the Christian community. "Oh, the Bible is culturally conditioned; meaning that when Paul rebuked homosexuality, prohibited women from serving as pastors, and ascribed creation to God instead of evolution, he was merely influenced by the traditional values of his age." Or, "It's fine to deny parts of Scripture as long as you accept the Bible as a whole."

Is it ever acceptable to compromise the word of God? No, which is why Jesus told the church at Pergamos, "Repent, or else I will come to you quickly and will fight against them with the sword of My mouth," Revelation 2:16. In other words, "You fix this, or I will." And the way to fix the problem in Pergamos—to defeat compromise—was, is, and always will be through wielding the sharp, doubled-edged sword of the Spirit, the Word of God.

As with each of the seven letters to the seven churches, Jesus closed His letter to Pergamos with the promise of victory: "To him who overcomes I will give some of the hidden manna to eat. And I will give him a white stone, and on the stone a new name written which no one knows except him who receives it," Revelation 2:17.

There are numerous suggestions as to the meaning of the "hidden manna" and "white stone." But perhaps the simplest explanation is the best. Manna refers to nourishment. A white stone with a new name refers to identity. Whatever we give up in life to remain faithful to Jesus, we can know with certainty that He will nourish us; that He will provide for us; that we belong to Him.

"He who has an ear, let him hear what the Spirit says to the churches."

# To Thyatira

Revelation 2:18-29

*"You allow that woman Jezebel, who calls herself a prophetess, to teach and seduce My servants."*

From Pergamos we travel forty-seven miles southeast to the church in Thyatira, a church impacted by worldliness.

## The City of Thyatira

Thyatira was the smallest of the seven cities in Revelation. It was not as prosperous as Ephesus, or as beautiful as Smyrna, or as politically connected as Pergamos. Pliny the Elder, a Roman author, dismissed Thyatira as "one of the unimportant communities of Asia." Yet, while Thyatira was never a metropolis of the ancient world, it was important commercially and militarily. And the reason for its importance was its location.

Thyatira was situated in the Lycus River Valley, forty-two miles from the Aegean Sea. It stood at the juncture of three great roads: the road to Pergamos, the road to Sardis, and the road to Smyrna. In antiquity these roads were important trade routes which, according to one historian, transported half of the world's goods.

Over time, Thyatira became a flourishing commercial center, known for its bronze and textiles, and especially for the production of purple dye. When the apostle Paul traveled from Asia Minor to Europe and entered Philippi, he met a woman named Lydia, who, according to Acts 16:14, was "a seller of purple from the city of Thyatira, who worshiped God."

Thyatira was also an important military city. The same roads that brought trade brought invading armies. As early as 290 B.C., Thyatira became a military outpost for the capital city of Pergamos some forty-seven miles away. As a first line of defense, Thyatira's role was not to repel invaders, but to delay them until Pergamos was prepared for battle. Militarily, then, Thyatira was a necessary city and an expendable city.

Unlike Ephesus, Smyrna, and Pergamos, Thyatira was not a major religious center. It contained temples dedicated to Apollo and Artemis, and a local religious celebrity known as the Sambathe. The Sambathe was an oracle or prophetess, who claimed to speak for Apollo, and for a fee foretold the future. Even fortune-telling was a thriving business in Thyatira.

In fact, Thyatira was so business oriented that it had more trade guilds than any other city in Asia Minor. Each guild had its own name, owned its own property, and wielded considerable economic and political power—similar to modern labor unions.

However, the trade guilds in Thyatira were not simply labor organizations. They were also religious organizations, combining commerce and worship, goods and gods. Each guild had its patron god. Guild meetings normally included prayers and sacrifices to pagan deities. Afterwards, sacrificed meat became the main course for a banquet. And the banquets quickly degenerated into drunken orgies. In Thyatira prostitution was a thriving business, too.

Was it possible for a Christian in Thyatira to belong to such a guild? Our immediate answer is, "No, of course not. God forbid." But what if failing to belong to a trade guild meant no paychecks, no groceries, and no mortgages? Wouldn't such financial need override the word and will of God? No.

In His letter to Thyatira, Jesus introduced Himself as "the Son of God, who has eyes like a flame of fire, and His feet like fine brass," Revelation 2:18. What was this picture meant to convey?

Have you ever seen a painting in which the eyes of a person—oh, those relentless eyes—follow you around the room; always watching, staring, penetrating? Even when you turn your back on the painting, you can feel the weight of those eyes. This is how Jesus painted Himself to the church in Thyatira. Eyes that were constantly watching. Flaming eyes that scorched away pretense, uncovered sin, and burned with anger at deliberate sin and deception and any harm done to His beloved churches.

This is not a painting of Jesus often seen on Sunday School materials or on Sunday bulletin covers, or for that matter, even in the gospels outside of Christ's memorable flashes of righteous anger at Israel's religious hypocrites or the moneychangers in the temple or even those disciples who tried to prevent little children from approaching Him. Most often we see the image of the Jesus with outstretched arms and a compassionate face. But those other eyes, the fiery and penetrating eyes, must be remembered too; lest anyone think that God does not care about sin or worldliness.

What did those penetrating eyes see in Thyatira? As troublesome as circumstances were, Jesus saw good things, too, and mentioned these first. Perhaps we could learn something from the Savior's approach. "I know your works, love, service, faith, and your patience," He said, "and as for your works, the last are more than the first," Revelation 2:19.

In some ways, the church at Thyatira was a model church. "Nevertheless," said Jesus, "I have a few things against you, because you allow that woman Jezebel, who calls herself a prophetess, to teach and seduce My servants to commit sexual immorality and eat things sacrificed to idols," Revelation 2:20.

Who was Jezebel? Some believe she was the local prophetess in Thyatira, the Sambathe. Others believe she was the pastor's wife. Most likely, the woman misleading believers in Thyatira was called *Jezebel* because she had all the traits of wicked Queen Jezebel in the Old Testament, who introduced Baal worship and its immorality into Israel. Even today we use the expression, "That woman is a Jezebel."

Note well: God did not call the Jezebel in Thyatira to be a prophetess. She called herself a prophetess, professing to speak for God. And anytime anyone appoints himself or herself to any teaching position in the church—apostle, prophet, pastor, teacher—and is not appointed by God, be on your guard.

The church in Pergamos also struggled with sexual immorality and food sacrificed to idols. However, the difference between the two congregations was this: believers in Pergamos were being influenced by false teachers outside of the congregation, while the false teaching in Thyatira came from within. "Because you *allow* that woman," said Jesus.

Someone once said, "When a church cracks, the world seeps in." This is what was happening in Thyatira. This is why the smallest city received the longest letter from Jesus. This is why the warning to that self-appointed Jezebel and against worldliness in churches was so strong. "And I gave her time to repent of her sexual immorality," said Jesus, "and she did not repent. Indeed I will cast her into a sickbed, and those who commit adultery with her into great tribulation, unless they repent of their deeds. I will kill her children with death, and all the churches shall know that I am He who searches the minds and hearts. And I will give to each one of you according to your works," Revelation 2:21-23.

Can a Christian be both worldly *and* godly? No. Conversely, if we, as Jesus said to the church in Thyatira, "hold fast what you have till I come," Revelation 2:25, if we overcome through Christ, if we strive to obey the will and word of Christ, we will one day rule with Christ in His eternal kingdom. As Jesus promised, "And he who overcomes, and keeps My works until the end, to him I will give power over the nations," Revelation 2:26.

"He who has an ear, let him hear what the Spirit says to the churches."

# To Sardis

## Revelation 3:1-6

*"Therefore if you will not watch, I will come upon you as a thief, and you will not know what hour I will come upon you."*

From Thyatira we travel thirty miles southeast to the church in Sardis, a church with a reputation for alertness, but in reality struggling with spiritual sleepiness.

### The City of Sardis

Sardis was one of the oldest, most powerful cities in Asia Minor. It was one of the wealthiest cities, too. Even today, the value of property is impacted by "location, location, location." This was certainly true of Sardis. While the city was sixty-three miles inland from the Aegean Sea, it stood at the juncture of five major roads: the road to Thyatira and Pergamos, the road to Smyrna, the road to Phrygia, the road to Philadelphia and Laodicea, and beyond them the many other towns of the Meander River Valley, and finally, the road to Ephesus and the Aegean Sea.

You may have heard the expression "as rich as Croesus." That expression is as ancient as Sardis. Croesus was the Bill Gates of antiquity, an extravagantly wealthy king who made Sardis the capital of Lydia. Under his administration, Sardis became the first city in the world to mint coins and use "money" in the modern sense of the term.

Sardis had all the amenities of a great, prosperous city: theater, music hall, library, a massive bath-and-gymnasium complex with a marble court, public buildings and beautiful residential homes, the famed Temple of Artemis (one of the seven wonders of the ancient world), and also the largest Jewish synagogue in antiquity—its dazzling mosaic floor still visible today in the ruins.

Additionally, Sardis was an important center of wool production and distribution, and like Thyatira, it specialized in dye-making. Jesus may have had this clothing aspect of Sardis in mind when he referred to "defiled garments" and "walking with Him in white.'"

Even nature contributed to the prosperity of Sardis. The area surrounding the city was rich with gold. The Pactolus River swept gold into the very heart of Sardis. According to myth, the Pactolus River became a source of gold only after the legendary King Midas, the man with the "golden touch," washed his hands in its waters.

Sardis was also known for its great defenses. According to some reports, the city was enclosed by a massive wall sixty-five feet wide and thirty feet tall. The Greek historian Polybius referred to Sardis as "the strongest place in the world."

Sardis, then, was a "happening place"—wealthy, powerful, boastful, and virtually invulnerable. In A.D. 17, when Sardis was leveled by an earthquake, the city was so prosperous and self-confident that it refused financial assistance from Emperor Tiberius. "We can do it ourselves," was the attitude. And yet, the same characteristics that brought Sardis fame wrought its eventual desolation. Like every other civilization in human history, including our own, Sardis began to decay from the inside out. Even pagans of that age contemptuously called Sardis a place of pleasure-loving and loose-living. To paraphrase the historian Herodotus, the residents of Sardis were only interested in pedicures, strumming the guitar, and selling retail.

Tragically, what was happening to the city of Sardis—an indifferent smugness, sleepiness, and complacency, a rot from the inside out—was also happening to the Christian congregation in Sardis. These were the circumstances Jesus addressed in His letter to Sardis, circumstances so dreadful that Sardis was one of only two churches in Revelation about which Jesus had nothing good to say.

## The Message to Sardis

The Savior's words to the church in Sardis contain many lessons for us. But let's focus on three.

First, everything about a Christian congregation is a gift from Jesus Christ. Notice how Jesus described Himself in the introduction of His letter to Sardis: "These things says He who has the seven Spirits of God and the seven stars," Revelation 3:1. The seven stars likely represent the seven "angels" or messengers of the seven churches; that is, their pastors. The "seven spirits" likely refer to the Holy Spirit with His sevenfold gifts—seven conveying the sense of completeness and perfection.

So from the outset, Jesus reminded the complacent, sleepy members of the church in Sardis, in effect, "I opened My hand and gave you your church, your pastor, and your faith through the working of My Holy Spirit and His sevenfold gifts. Realize how precious these gifts are. Realize also that these gifts, if despised, can be taken away." Surely, this is a reason for remaining spiritually active and alert.

Second, Jesus does not see churches as we do. This may be a surprising and sobering thought to church councils and planning committees, but it is absolutely true. Jesus reminded the church in Ephesus, "I walk back and forth amid the people and pews of your congregation." He reminded the church in Smyrna, "I know your suffering," and the church in Pergamos, "I know where you live." He reminded the church in Thyatira of His flaming eyes that see everything. Read all seven letters to the seven churches and count the number of times Jesus says "I know."

When the residents of Sardis looked at the Christian church in Sardis, indeed, when the members of the church looked at themselves, they saw a "happening church in a happening city." Jesus saw something else. "You have a name that you are alive," He said in Revelation 3:1, "but you are dead."

Plastic flowers may look stunningly beautiful and

realistic, but they are dead, too. Such was the case in Sardis. The church there had a reputation for living, growing, flourishing, blossoming; of being the place to attend for Sunday worship. And yet, when Jesus looked at that place-to-be church, He saw death. "You are dead," He said. A church can have the appearance of life, but nevertheless be dead on the inside. Why? Because the emphasis is no longer on the life-giving Word of God, no longer on the essential knowledge of sin and grace, but has shifted instead to externals. If the Word of God is absent or unimportant, how can faith live? How can a church live?

Third, Jesus offered the church in Sardis the solution for its spiritual sleepiness. And notice all the strong imperatives He used in Revelation 3:2-3. *Be watchful. Strengthen. Remember. Hold fast. Repent.* Surely, "be watchful" and "strengthen" belong together. For the only way to wake up and strengthen faith is through the Word of God.

"Remember," "hold fast," and "repent" belong together, too. Whether personal life or church life, the temptation is always to turn from Scripture to something new, something different. Nonsense. The means to overcome, as Jesus stated to all seven churches, is never to turn from God's Word, but always to turn to God's Word.

Above all, let's never assume that we can do without the Word of God. The words are sobering, but also necessary to hear: "Therefore if you will not watch, I will come upon you as a thief, and you will not know what hour I will come upon you," Revelation 3:3. Conversely, along with the warning, Jesus made this glorious promise: "He who overcomes shall be clothed in white garments, and I will not blot out his name from the Book of Life; but I will confess his name before My Father and before His angels," Revelation 3:5.

"He who has an ear, let him hear what the Spirit says to the churches."

# To Philadelphia

Revelation 3:7-13

*"I have set before you an open door, and no one can shut it."*

From Sardis we travel thirty miles southeast to the church in Philadelphia, a church with little strength.

## The City of Philadelphia

Long before Philadelphia, Pennsylvania, there was a Philadelphia in Asia Minor, established in 189 B.C. by King Eumenes of Lydia, who named the city *Philadelphia* to honor his younger brother, Attalus II. *Philadelphia* comes from two Greek words: *PHILOS*, meaning love or affection; and *ADELPHOS*, meaning brother. Hence, the city of brotherly love.

Ancient Philadelphia stood on a low, broad hill near the base of Mount Tmolus—the same mountain which spawned the river that swept gold into the marketplace of Sardis. Situated on a major trade route, Philadelphia became very wealthy. Its prosperity was also enhanced by its products: wool, textiles, leather, and especially wine made from grapes grown in the rich volcanic soil of the lush vineyards. The vineyards resulted in a booming wine industry, as well as the worship of Dionysus, the Greek god of wine, agriculture, fertility, and performing arts.

Built on a hill, and with a commanding view of the Hermus River Valley, Philadelphia was easily defended and important militarily. And yet, the same location that brought the city enormous wealth also brought it enormous danger. Philadelphia was founded directly over a seismic fault; and in A.D. 17 was completely destroyed by a major earthquake— the same earthquake that leveled Sardis. However, unlike

Sardis, Philadelphia experienced ongoing earthquakes and aftershocks for more than twenty years.

According to one biblical commentator, no other city in Asia Minor suffered more violent and recurring earthquakes. In fact, the ancient historian Strabo, who lived 64 B.C. to A.D. 21, wrote of Philadelphia, "Philadelphia has no trustworthy walls, but daily in one direction or another they keep tottering and falling apart."

Philadelphia, then, was a city "on the edge," a city with jittery nerves, a city always expecting The Big One. Amid such shaky circumstances, how comforting these words of Jesus must have been: "He who overcomes, I will make him a pillar in the temple of My God, and he shall go out no more," Revelation 3:12. A pillar. A word suggesting strength and stability. As if an enduring testimony to this promise of Jesus, one of the few things still standing in the ruins of Philadelphia is the pillar of an ancient church.

## The Church in Philadelphia

While we don't know who founded the First Christian Church of Philadelphia, we can learn much about this congregation from the letter it received from Jesus Christ. In many respects, the Philadelphian church was remarkably like the church in Smyrna. Both were suffering churches. Both were persecuted by hateful, hostile Jews, those whom Jesus described in His letters to Smyrna and Philadelphia as a "synagogue of Satan."

The churches in Smyrna and Philadelphia were also the only two churches in Revelation to receive no rebuke from the risen Christ. Said differently, the two churches that suffered the most experienced the fewest spiritual problems. Is there a connection?

According to Jesus, the church in Philadelphia was also a little church, a struggling church. "For you have a little strength," said Jesus in Revelation 3:8. Little strength. Little membership. Little budget. Little statistics. Little prospect.

What did Jesus want this little church in Philadelphia to see?

## The Message to Philadelphia

First, Jesus is the One who opens and closes doors for a church ministry. This is critical to realize. Too often we convince ourselves that we're the ones who open doors and create opportunities for church growth; that we're the ones who attain success through careful planning, perfect timing, and massive budgets. The opposite is true.

Jesus said to the Christians in Philadelphia, "I have set before you an open door, and no one can shut it," Revelation 3:8. He made the door. He opened the door. If an opportunity is not from the Lord, it is destined to fail. And no amount of money, pushing, pleading, or banging will make the door open. Conversely, if an opportunity is from the Lord, then no matter how small a congregation's membership, resources, or budget, the opportunity will succeed.

Second, when the Lord opens a door of opportunity, He will give us the strength and wisdom to walk through it. Nearly every Sunday, as part of our worship service, we recite the Lord's Prayer. In concluding we say, "For thine is the kingdom and the power and the glory forever and ever." And then we exit church, turn right or left toward the next intersection and next problem, and begin to worry as if we didn't believe a single word we prayed. O Lord God, forgive us. Help us see Your power at work in our church and our lives.

Frankly, I always bristle when I hear well-intentioned people declare at evangelism seminars or revivals, "God needs you to spread the gospel. God needs you as a worker in His kingdom. God needs you to win people for Jesus." No He doesn't. God doesn't need anything from us. We need *Him*.

Imagine how overwhelmed and intimidated that little church in Philadelphia was by the opposition of hostile Jews, by the worldliness of city-life in Philadelphia, by the presence of pagan temples, and by the threat of earthquakes and aftershocks. And yet, each time Jesus asked something of these believers in His letter, He directed them to the absolute source of power, success, and protection; namely, Himself. "*I* have set before you," Revelation 3:8. "*I* will make them," 3:9; "*I* also will keep you," 3:10. "*I* am coming quickly," 3:11. "*I* will make him," 3:12. "*I* will write on him," 3:12.

Third, Jesus opens and closes doors for us as individuals, too. How many doors? Too many to count. The Lord opened the door of life to you when He formed you in your mother's womb. The Lord opened the door of new life and eternal life to you when He led you to faith in Jesus Christ—Who, speaking of doors, said of Himself in John 10:9, "I am the door. If anyone enters by Me, he will be saved, and will go in and out and find pasture." And in John 14:6, "I am the way, the truth, and the life. No one comes to the Father except through Me."

And when the Lord closes the door on this earthly life, He will open the door to eternal life; the life that will never end, and the door that will never close. The eternal life Jesus pictured in His letter to Philadelphia by saying, "He who overcomes, I will make him a pillar in the temple of My God, and he shall go out no more," Revelation 3:12.

Doors, blessings, opportunities from God; perhaps best summarized by the words Jesus spoke to the church in Laodicea. Words which Jesus says to each of us: "Behold, I stand at the door and knock. If anyone hears My voice and opens the door, I will come in to him and dine with him, and he with Me," Revelation 3:20. Christ's voice, His Word, is that which opens the door and creates faith.

"He who has an ear, let him hear what the Spirit says to the churches."

# To Laodicea

Revelation 3:14-22

*"I know your works, that you are neither cold nor hot. I could wish you were cold or hot. So then, because you are lukewarm . . ."*

From Philadelphia we travel forty-eight miles southeast to Laodicea and the last of the seven churches, a church with a lukewarm love for God.

## The City of Laodicea

The city was originally called Diospolis, then Rhoas. But in 260 B.C., King Antiochus II of Syria renamed the city Laodicea to honor his wife Laodice. Laodicea was located in the Lycus River Valley. Situated on two great trade routes, Laodicea became a flourishing commercial center and acquired enormous wealth. That wealth was reflected in the city's architecture, population, and attractions.

For example, while some ancient cities struggled to support even one theater, Laodicea had two: one with 8,000 seats and another with 15,000 seats. And in wealthy Laodicea, theater seats were inscribed with the names of their owners. Along with two theaters, Laodicea boasted a 40,000-seat amphitheater, with room for an additional 15,000 spectators on its north slope—nearly the same seating capacity as Dodger Stadium in Los Angeles.

There were magnificent temples; public baths, spas, and gymnasiums; markets and stores; expensive art exhibits; a famous medical school; an odeum for concerts and lectures; a bouleuterion or city council chambers; and streets lined with columns and pedestals. In fact, Main Street in Laodicea was equipped with a subterranean sewer system that swept away waste water from homes and businesses.

Laodicea was so wealthy that when an earthquake devastated the city in A.D. 60, its residents refused all financial assistance from imperial Rome. "No thanks," they said. "We have everything we need. We're rich. We don't want your help."

In antiquity, Laodicea was especially known for three items: banks, fabrics, and eye salve. Banks were a natural consequence of the city's wealth, trade, and tourism. The fabrics for which Laodicea was famous were made from the glossy black wool of local sheep. The wool was used to make warm, waterproof garments that were highly prized and high priced in the Roman world.

Laodicean eye salve was developed by the city's medical school. The salve was composed of ground stone, mixed with water, turned into salve, and applied to the eyelids. Long before bifocals, contact lenses, and Lasik Surgery, people throughout the ancient world bought Laodicean eye salve to improve poor vision.

And yet, despite all of its wealth and civic pride, Laodicea had one glaring weakness: The city had no local water source. Water was transported via aqueduct from hots springs near the city of Hierapolis, six miles away. The water was so rich with minerals, especially calcium, that it frequently clogged the stone pipes in the aqueduct. Even worse, by the time the water reached Laodicea, it was lukewarm. Imagine drinking a "refreshing" cup of chalky, lukewarm Laodicean water.

## The Church in Laodicea

Laodicea was only nine miles from Colossae. When Paul wrote his letter to the Colossians, he mentioned the Laodiceans four times; and by doing so, provided a brief description of the Laodicean church as it existed in A.D. 61. A small but thriving church. A church meeting in the home of a woman named Nympha. A church being served by Pastor Epaphras from Colossae. A Scripture-oriented, Christ-centered, and Spirit-empowered church.

Sadly, move forward thirty-four years to A.D. 95 and the time of Revelation, and we find a remarkably different First Christian Church of Laodicea, a church about which Jesus had nothing good to say, a church for which Jesus reserved one of His harshest rebukes: "So then, because you are lukewarm, and neither cold nor hot, I will vomit you out of My mouth," Revelation 3:16.

As we read the Savior's letter to Laodicea, we discover a Christian congregation barely distinguishable from its worldly surroundings. Is that what Jesus intended when He called His disciples "lights of the world" and "salt of the earth"? Did Jesus intend for Christian congregations to imitate the world, or to change the world? We know the answer. Paul wrote in Romans 12:2, "And do not be conformed to this world, but be transformed by the renewing of your mind, that you may prove what is that good and acceptable and perfect will of God."

Yet, the First Christian Church of Laodicea had come to share many of the characteristics of the city in which it resided. The city claimed to be rich, and so did its Christian church. "You say, 'I am rich,'" Revelation 3:17. The city refused help from its Lord Caesar, just as the Laodicean church refused help from its Lord Christ. The city had lukewarm water, and its Christian church had a lukewarm attitude toward Christ.

## The Message to Laodicea

"Because you say, 'I am rich, have become wealthy, and have need of nothing,'" Revelation 3:17. In wealthy Laodicea, this boast of the Laodicean church was likely true. It did have wealth. It did have resources. It did have impressive statistics and fine furnishings and a rapidly growing membership, and over time, it apparently came to believe that having such externalities was more important than having Christ. When the worship service ended, which conversation was more animated: talk about Jesus or talk about the latest art exhibit, the next concert, or the next gladiatorial event at Laodicea's 40,000-seat amphitheater?

This is the deceptiveness of wealth: the belief that when one has money, he has the means to happiness. And so Jesus, the Amen, the always faithful Lord, told the Laodiceans the truth about themselves, that is, who and what they truly were by nature and apart from Him: "Because you say, I am rich, have become wealthy, and have need of nothing—and do not know that you are wretched, miserable, poor, blind, and naked," Revelation 3:17.

According to Scripture, this is true of all of us. No matter how famous, powerful, wealthy, keen-sighted, or well-dressed we are, by nature we are wretched, pitiful, beggarly, blind, and naked. If we see ourselves as we are by nature, and if we understand that in pure, undeserved grace Jesus Christ laid down His priceless life to save us, how can we become or remain lukewarm toward God?

As Jesus explained, the solution to lukewarm Christianity is to repent, to understand the limitations of earthly wealth and the lost-ness of human nature, and to find true riches in Christ. "I counsel you to buy from Me gold refined in the fire, that you may be rich; and white garments, that you may be clothed that the shame of your nakedness may not be revealed; and anoint your eyes with salve, that you may see," Revelation 3:18.

All of us wish for a life free from problems. No disease. No loss. No pain. Yet, it is precisely when things go well for us, as they did for the church in Laodicea, that we are in the most danger of growing lukewarm toward God. The Lord Jesus is never lukewarm toward us, but wants only the most personal of relationships with us. "Behold," He said, I stand at the door and knock. If anyone hears My voice and opens the door, I will come in to him and dine with him, and he with Me," Revelation 3:20.

"He who has an ear, let him hear what the Spirit says to the churches."

# <u>Seven Words</u>

# Forgiveness

## Luke 23:34

*"Father, forgive them, for they do not know what they do."*

Scripture describes the crucifixion of Jesus Christ in brief and relatively "bloodless" terms. Yet, we know from ancient historians and modern archaeological excavations how brutal, gruesome, and bloody crucifixion was. Reserved for the vilest of criminals and the lowest of slaves, crucifixion was designed to be excruciatingly painful. In fact, our English word *excruciating* is from the Latin word *excruciatus*, literally meaning "out of the cross."

And the pain of the cross lasted for hours, at times even days. The physical tortures were unspeakable. In Roman crucifixions, five- to seven-inch iron spikes were driven through the wrists and feet. With no other support for the weight of the body, shoulders, elbows, and wrists became dislocated, something which was spoken prophetically about Jesus in Psalm 22, a psalm with many references to Christ's crucifixion: "I am poured out like water, and all My bones are out of joint," Psalm 22:14.

The position of the body on the cross made it nearly impossible to breathe, particularly to exhale. The only way to exhale completely was to pull oneself up on the cross, putting weight on the iron spikes in both hands and feet. Consequently, death on a cross was often related to suffocation. And along with the physical torture of crucifixion came the psychological torture of constantly gasping for breath and, in many cases, the public shame of being crucified naked.

Though we read the Passion History of our Lord and Savior, we have no real conception of what He suffered on the cross. His physical suffering was gruesome enough. But at the same time, He was carrying the weight of the world's sins and experiencing the agonies of hell itself: "And the LORD has laid on Him the iniquity of us all," Isaiah 53:6.

Under such dreadful circumstances, how difficult it must have been for the crucified Jesus to speak. And yet, according to the gospels, Jesus did speak seven times while hanging on the cross; not curses or regrets or desperate pleas for mercy; rather, words of love, forgiveness, compassion, agony, and victory.

His first words from the cross were "Father, forgive them, for they do not know what they do," Luke 23:34.

Consider the setting for these words. When we speak of forgiveness, the setting is often church: pews, hymns, readings, smiles, handshakes, and the thermostat set at a comfortable seventy degrees. But this was not the setting in which Jesus spoke words of forgiveness.

Recall the Passion History; how the night before His crucifixion, Jesus was arrested, then interrogated for hours by Caiaphas the High Priest, Pilate the Roman Governor, and Herod the Jewish King. Afterwards, Roman soldiers mocked, scorned, and spit on Jesus, and then beat Him to the point of disfigurement—something prophesied by Isaiah seven hundred years before it happened. Isaiah 52:14, "So His visage was marred more than any man, and His form more than the sons of men."

Then Jesus was dressed in a royal purple robe and crowned with thorns, the very symbol of the curse that fell on the earth after Adam and Eve fell into sin. "Cursed is the ground for your sake; in toil you shall eat of it all the days of your life. Both thorns and thistles it shall bring forth for you," Genesis 3:17-18. And so, adorned in purple and crowned with thorns, Jesus was paraded before a frenzied mob, who preferred Barabbas the Killer to Jesus the Christ.

Then Jesus was flogged with the dreaded Roman flagellum, a whip made of leather straps tipped with jagged metal or sharp stones—an instrument of torture which literally tore flesh from bone. And on that torn flesh, Jesus was forced to carry His own cross to His own execution. And once at Golgotha, the Place of the Skull, Jesus was nailed to the cross. We can almost, almost, hear the hammer blows.

Yet, dear reader, even when Jesus was falsely accused, unjustly condemned, and finally nailed to the cross, His first words were words of forgiveness and compassion. He did not curse. He did not revile. He did not descend from the cross and annihilate those who were killing Him, though He had every right, reason, and power to do so. He did not pray, "Father, obliterate them, for they deserve it." And they did deserve it, as we deserve it by nature.

Rather than think of Himself, Jesus thought first of us. Jesus spoke first of the world He came to save. And He prayed, "Father, forgive them, for they do not know what they do."

"Father," said Jesus. His words were a prayer. His place of prayer was the cross. In dire circumstances we often pray for ourselves: "Father, save my life." "Father, save my marriage." "Father, save me from this illness." "Father, save me from myself." But when we suffer *because* of others, how often is our first response to pray for them? Yet, this is exactly what Jesus did on the cross. In fact, on Mount Calvary Jesus put into practice the very principles He preached on the Mount of Beatitudes: "Love your enemies, bless those who curse you, do good to those who hate you, and pray for those who spitefully use you and persecute you," Matthew 5:44.

Consequently, the "them" and "they" of Christ's first words from the cross were spoken on behalf of those who abused Him, mistreated Him, hated Him, and crucified Him. The Roman soldiers who joked while driving the nails. The religious leaders who perverted God's law, yet accused Jesus of blasphemy. Pontius Pilate, who, knowing Christ's innocence, washed his hands of the injustice. The Jews who plotted against Jesus. The two thieves crucified with Jesus, both of whom initially reviled and cursed Him. The steady stream of travelers who came to Golgotha to satisfy their curiosity and hurl their insults: "If you are the Son of God, come down from the cross," Matthew 27:40.

To all those people who participated in Christ's death, surely His words applied: "For they do not know what they do." This was not an excuse, but simply the reality. They didn't know, but they should have known. And they didn't know because they didn't believe. Yet, even for them Jesus prayed, "Father, forgive them." He uttered these first words from the cross, because forgiveness was what He first and foremost came to bring.

When Jesus prayed, "Father forgive them," He was also praying for each of us. No, we're not the ones who condemned Jesus to die. We're not the ones who crowned Him with thorns or bludgeoned Him with fists or rolled dice for His garments or laughed at His misery. But make no mistake: We are as responsible for Christ's crucifixion as Pilate, Herod, Caiaphas, and the Roman legionnaires who hammered the nails. For it was Christ's desire to atone for *our* sins, too, that compelled Him to the cross. And it was love, not rusty Roman nails, that held Him there.

Yet, on the cross, Jesus not only prayed for our forgiveness; through that very cross Jesus obtained our forgiveness. And for people who, despite the best of intentions, daily sin against God in thought, word, and deed, can there be anything more important or more comforting than the blessed knowledge that through the sacrifice of Jesus Christ all our sins have been forgiven?

And so we humbly and gratefully say with the apostle Paul, "In Him we have redemption through His blood, the forgiveness of sins, according to the riches of His grace," Ephesians 1:7.

"Father, forgive them." Jesus speaks. Do we hear Him?

# Paradise

## Luke 23:43

*"Assuredly, I say to you, today you will be with Me in Paradise."*

The first words Jesus spoke from the cross conveyed forgiveness: "Father, forgive them." When He spoke a second time, He offered hope, acceptance, and forgiveness to a dying, penitent thief. "Assuredly, I say to you, today you will be with Me in Paradise," Luke 23:43.

The Bible does not name the two thieves crucified with Jesus; but it does describe them as "criminals" in Luke 23:32 and as "robbers" in Matthew 27:38. These were not men who stole by craftiness or stealth, but men who robbed by violence, brutality, and even murder. The same Greek word for "robber" is used in the *Parable of the Good Samaritan* to describe the robbers who viciously beat a traveler, stole his clothes and belongings, and left him half-dead on a deserted highway.

Yet, in the last pitiful hours of his life, one of these hardened criminals came to faith in Jesus, confessed his sins, pleaded for God's mercy, and heard the Savior reply: "Assuredly, I say to you, today you will be with Me in Paradise." What may we learn from these words of Christ from the cross?

### The Truthfulness of God's Word

This is no small lesson. Most of us know the story of the two thieves crucified with Jesus; particularly, the one thief to whom Jesus said, "Today you will be with me in Paradise." But how many of us know that this very event was foretold by Scripture?

More than seven centuries before the birth of Jesus, God said through the prophet Isaiah, "Therefore I will divide Him a portion with the great, and He shall divide the spoil with the strong, because He poured out His soul unto death, *and He was numbered with the transgressors*, and He bore the sin of many, and made intercession for the transgressors," Isaiah 53:12.

Jesus was numbered with the transgressors when He was crucified with two thieves. And Jesus certainly made intercession for transgressors, including all of us, when He prayed "Father, forgive them" from the cross. Like every other aspect of redemptive history, even the death of Jesus alongside criminals is a testament to the truthfulness of God's Word. As stated in Mark 15:27-28, "With Him they also crucified two robbers, one on His right and the other on His left. So the Scripture was fulfilled which says, 'And He was numbered with the transgressors.' "

God keeps His word. And this should give us enormous comfort. For when we turn to the Scriptures for answers for the Here-And-Now and the Here-After, for heartache, loneliness, loss, sickness, or a troubled marriage, we know that we are reading God's absolute truth. We know that what God promises us He will most certainly do for us.

## The Centrality of Christ and His Cross

All four gospels mention that two others were crucified with Jesus, one on His right, one on His left. But why was the cross of Jesus in the center? Was the location a matter of coincidence or convenience, an arbitrary order of Pontius Pilate, or even his attempt to irk the Jews by showcasing the Christ? We're not told. Yet, would the almighty, all-knowing God leave any aspect of His redemptive plan—anything pertaining to the crucifixion of His own Son, Jesus Christ, including the placement of His cross—to mere coincidence?

No. God does not do coincidences, but is rather the God Who, according to Ephesians 1:11, "works all things according to the counsel of His will."

Perhaps the cross of Jesus was in the center because His

cross is central to our eternal salvation, and to such an extent that there can be no salvation without the crucifixion of Jesus.

When many churches today, even Christian churches, are removing the word *sin* from their sermons and crosses from their sanctuaries, in clear opposition to such practices Paul told the Corinthians, "For I determined not to know anything among you except Jesus Christ and Him crucified," 1 Corinthians 2:2.

Or perhaps the cross of Jesus was in the center, one thief on the right and one thief on the left, to show how near God's salvation was to both; and how one thief reviled and rejected Jesus, while the other received Jesus and was saved.

So it has ever been and ever will be: Christ at the center. As in the Book of Revelation, Christ at the center of the throne of God. Christ at the center of time and eternity. Christ at the center of God's redemptive plan to deliver lost mankind. Christ Who came to save and will come again to judge. Christ Who can be reviled or received, but not avoided. And so we read in John 3:18, "He who believes in Him is not condemned; but He who does not believe is condemned already, because He has not believed in the name of the only begotten Son of God."

### The Magnificence of God's Grace

Jesus told the penitent thief: "Assuredly, I say to you, today you will be with Me in Paradise." We have the same words and the same promise, because we have the same Savior and the same salvation—a salvation that is due solely to God's grace in Jesus Christ, apart from who we are or what we do or what we own.

"You will be with Me," said Jesus. To whom was He speaking? A man known for leading a godly life? No. Jesus was addressing a man who had robbed, hurt, and possibly murdered; a man who in the last desperate hours of his miserable life turned to the very Savior he had previously reviled and humbly pleaded, "Lord, remember me when You come into Your kingdom," Luke 23:42.

Why would Jesus Christ, the Son of God, want to remember a person like that; or for that matter, a person like you or me? The answer is grace, that is, God's undeserved love in Christ Jesus. Grace, which has nothing to do with who we are and everything to do with Who God is.

The penitent thief was not saved because he was worthy, but despite his unworthiness. He was not saved because of his works—works which had been evil, or because of his possessions. Everything he owned and thought worth stealing was by this time divided among Roman soldiers or waiting for him in a pauper's grave. On that cross, on that Friday, he had no wallet, no money, no pockets, no clothes. His hands were empty, except for the nails.

No, this man was saved by God's grace, just as we are, of which Paul wrote, "For by grace you have been saved through faith, and that not of yourselves; it is the gift of God, not of works, lest anyone should boast," Ephesians 2:8-9.

Someone once observed—and I'm paraphrasing, "Perhaps God included the story of the penitent thief in Scripture so that we will neither presume nor despair." As for presumption, that we will never take God's grace for granted, foolishly assuming there will always be another day, another opportunity to embrace Christ as Lord and Savior. There may not be. There were no future opportunities for the two thieves on the cross. One believed. One did not.

And as for despairing, that we will never think we are too lost to be found, too sinful to be forgiven, or too late to be saved. Rather, that despite all our ills and heartaches, our sins and failures, we, like that penitent thief, turn to the crucified Savior, confess our sins, rely on His mercy, and hear His gracious words: "Assuredly, I say to you, today you will be with Me in Paradise,"

"Today. With Me. Paradise."

Jesus speaks. Do we hear Him?

# Family

John 19:26-27

*"When Jesus therefore saw His mother, and the disciple whom He loved standing by, He said to His mother, 'Woman, behold your son!' Then He said to the disciple, 'Behold your mother!' And from that hour that disciple took her to his own home."*

Only five days earlier, thousands upon thousands lined the streets of Jerusalem to welcome the approaching King. They shouted hosannas. They waved palm branches. They carpeted the road with garments. They sang, "Blessed is the King who comes in the name of the LORD! Peace in heaven and glory in the highest!" Luke 19:38.

Yet, after the strange glory of Palm Sunday came the blackness of Good Friday. As Jesus hung on the cross, no one praised or welcomed Him. No one shouted hosannas. Not Simon Peter, who had said, "Lord, I am ready to go with You, both to prison and to death," Luke 22:33. Not Thomas, who had said, "Let us also go, that we may die with Him," John 11:16. Not Zacchaeus the tax collector, or even one of the multitudes of the sick, crippled, and dying whom Jesus had graciously healed. The Savior was, as Isaiah described Him, "despised and rejected by men, a Man of sorrows and acquainted with grief," Isaiah 53:3.

Indeed, on that Good Friday, as Roman soldiers went about their bloody work and curious travelers paused at Golgotha to revile and spit, perhaps only four disciples stood near the cross of Jesus, one man and three women: John, the brother of James; Mary, the wife of Clopas; Mary of Magdala; and Mary, the mother of Jesus.

We can almost see them huddling together in the

lengthening shadow of the cross: weeping, hopeless and helpless, eyes repeatedly drawn to the crucified Savior. We see the nails, wounds, blood, and crown of thorns, the public notice written in Greek, Latin, Hebrew, and of course Sarcasm: JESUS OF NAZARETH, THE KING OF THE JEWS. For most, this superscription was no more than the punchline of a bad joke, a joke about a silly Jewish rabbi, Who thought He was the Son of God and Savior of Mankind. HA-HA-HA.

Standing close to the cross, the small band of disciples had already heard the Savior speak twice: speak for the world, "Father, forgive them," and speak to a penitent thief, "Today you will be with Me in Paradise."

Yet, as dreadful as this scene was for John, for Mary the wife of Clopas, and for Mary of Magdala; surely, it must have been unbearable for Mary the mother of Jesus. What went through her mind as she watched the agonies of her Son and her Savior? As she heard His last words, did she recall His first steps, or that first Christmas when she had wrapped Him in swaddling clothes? Did she recall His little hands in hers, the same hands now nailed to the cross?

But then, looking up at Jesus, Mary saw Him looking down at her. And despite His agony and pain, He spoke a third time from the cross. "When Jesus therefore saw His mother, and the disciple whom He loved standing by, He said to His mother, 'Woman, behold your son!' Then He said to the disciple, 'Behold your mother!' And from that hour that disciple took her to his own home," John 19:26-27.

"Behold your son." "Behold your mother." Tender, heartwarming words. Yet, compared to the other words Jesus spoke from the cross—words about forgiveness, Paradise, being forsaken by God, thirsting for God, the "it is finished" of our salvation, and the "Father, into Your hands" spoken when Jesus willingly surrendered His life—His words to Mary and John may seem trivial, a family matter that Jesus understandably forgot to arrange amid His betrayal, arrest, scourging, and crucifixion.

But is this really the case? Are we to believe that Jesus Christ, true God and true Man, forgot to care for His mother until He unexpectedly saw her standing beneath His cross?

No. The words Jesus spoke to Mary and John that Good Friday were not a postscript or an afterthought. Jesus spoke these words—ultimately, words about caring, sharing, and family—while on the cross because the words derive their greatest meaning from the cross of Jesus, as do all other aspects of the Christian life. Loving. Serving. Forgiving. Healing.

"Behold your son." "Behold your mother." Yes, these words were spoken specifically to Mary and John. But because of the cross of Jesus, they have great meaning for us, too.

### God Cares About Every Aspect of Our Lives

When we think of God—our infinite, all-knowing, all-powerful God—we generally think of big things and big accomplishments: the creation of the universe, the governance of nations, the parting of the Red Sea, the raising of Lazarus. And certainly, we think of the BIG THINGS Jesus obtained for us on the cross: forgiveness, eternal life, eternal salvation, an eternal inheritance. Yet, when it comes to the littler things of life, the ordinary needs and daily pressures, we're not always as certain of God's involvement. "No, God has better things to do and better places to be."

Yet, the words Jesus spoke from the cross insist otherwise. While He was bleeding and dying for the sins of humanity, He still made the time to provide for His mother. At His cross, Jesus provided for Mary's eternal salvation and also her daily bread.

### God is Willing to Help

What if Mary, the mother of Jesus, had left the cross on Good Friday, thinking, "I'm so grateful Jesus wants to provide for my daily needs, but I'm not certain He actually will." You and I would call such a perspective absurd. You and I would say, "But Mary, you were standing beneath the cross. You saw the nails, blood, wounds, crown of thorns, and superscription. You heard Jesus say 'Father, forgive them' and 'It is finished.' If Jesus was willing to die for your sins, why would He be unwilling to help you with anything else?"

I'm certain Mary never entertained such thoughts. I'm equally certain that I have. Haven't you? "I've lost my job, but I doubt that God will help." "My marriage is in trouble, but I doubt that God will help." In view of the cross, aren't such thoughts absurd, too? If the Savior died to accomplish our eternal salvation, will He deny us a loaf of bread or a change of clothes or a place to live?

### God Has the Power to Mend Broken Families

This is true at many levels. Mary and John were not related, but at the cross of Jesus they became a family and accepted the responsibility of caring for each other. Why? Not because they owed each other anything, but because they owed their Lord and Savior everything.

In the same way, the cross of Jesus makes one Christian Church out of many different nations, peoples, and cultures. All Christians are blood-relatives; not because of their blood, but because of Christ's blood. As Paul wrote, "For you are all sons of God through faith in Christ Jesus. For as many as were baptized into Christ have put on Christ. There is neither Jew nor Greek, there is neither slave nor free, there is neither male nor female; for you are all one in Christ Jesus," Galatians 3:26-28. At the cross of Jesus, Mary and John became a family. At the cross of Jesus, we find healing for our families, too.

"Behold your son. Behold your mother."

Jesus speaks. Do we hear Him?

# Forsaken

Matthew 27:45-46

*"Now from the sixth hour until the ninth hour there
was darkness over all the land. And about the ninth
hour Jesus cried out with a loud voice, saying, 'Eli,
Eli, lama sabachthani?' that is, 'My God, My God,
why have You forsaken Me?'"*

According to the gospels, Jesus was crucified at 9:00 A.M.
on Good Friday—by Jewish reckoning, the third hour of the
day. His crucifixion came after hours of no food and no sleep;
after brutal interrogations by Pilate, Herod, and Caiaphas;
after being mocked, slapped, spit upon, scourged, dressed in
royal purple, crowned with thorns, and forced to carry His
own cross, until bleeding and exhausted, He finally stumbled
beneath its weight.

During His first three hours on the cross, 9:00 A.M. to
12:00 noon, Jesus spoke three times; spoke despite the
agonizing pain and the constant struggle to breathe. He prayed
for the sinful world, saying, "Father, forgive them, for they
know not what they do." He offered forgiveness and
acceptance to a dying, penitent thief, saying, "Assuredly, I say
to you, today you will be with Me in Paradise." He addressed
His mother Mary and His disciple John, saying to Mary,
"Behold your son," and to John, "Behold your mother."

But from the sixth hour to the ninth hour, 12:00 noon to
3:00 P.M., Jesus said nothing. We can only imagine what He
was thinking and feeling. During those same three hours, a
dreadful darkness covered all the land, and perhaps even all
the earth.

It was then, in that darkness, near 3:00 P.M., that Jesus
spoke a fourth time from the cross, though "spoke" is too

small a word. He didn't merely speak. He cried out with a loud voice, asking, "Eli, Eli, lama sabachthani?" Aramaic for "My God, My God, why have You forsaken Me?" What did these words mean for Jesus? What do they mean for us?

## Fulfilled Scripture

When Jesus cried out, "My God, My God, why have You forsaken Me?"—He was fulfilling Scripture. In fact, He was quoting directly from Psalm 22:1, which reads in its entirety, "My God, My God, why have You forsaken Me? Why are You so far from helping Me, and from the words of My groaning?"

The Hebrew word for *groaning* in Psalm 22:1 literally means "to roar," and is used elsewhere in the Old Testament to describe the loud roar of a lion. King David used the same word in Psalm 32:3 to portray his own loud cries of anguish and wretchedness resulting from unrepented sin: "When I kept silent, my bones grew old through my groaning all the day long."

On the cross, then, Jesus not only fulfilled Scripture by quoting Psalm 22:1, He did so in the same type of voice described in this psalm. A roaring voice. Or as stated in the gospels, "with a loud voice." A voice filled with anguish, wretchedness, and pain.

"My God, My God, why have You forsaken Me?" Though the words are filled with untold misery and pain, in them we see yet another example—indeed, one of the most glorious examples—of how Almighty God keeps His word and fulfills His promises. And tell me, is there anything more comforting in a world of meaningless words and broken promises and fine-print disclaimers?

Jesus promised to die on the cross and He kept that promise. What should such love and faithfulness mean to us? In blessedly practical terms, it means that if God has promised to save you, He will. If God has promised to deliver you in times of trouble, He will. If God has promised to forgive your sins whenever you turn to Him in repentance and faith, He will. If God has promised to enrich your troubled marriage, He will. If God has promised to bring you safely from grace to glory, from this life to the next, He will.

How do you know this? Because God is faithful. Because God takes His word seriously, even when we do not. And the proof is in the cross of Jesus—in that loud roar of pain and wretchedness: "My God, My God, why have You forsaken Me?"

## Promised Messiah

When Jesus cried out, "My God, My God, why have You forsaken Me?"—He was also identifying Himself as the long-awaited Messiah. In quoting Psalm 22:1, Jesus was not only fulfilling Scripture, Scripture was being fulfilled in Him.

Most Jews in Israel, and certainly every priest and Levite in Jerusalem, understood that Psalm 22 was about the coming Messiah. Yet, though they knew, many refused to believe that Jesus was that Messiah or that they themselves had condemned their Messiah to the cross. And in doing so, they had no excuse. Throughout His three-and-a-half-year ministry, Jesus repeatedly revealed His identity as the Messiah in powerful words and miraculous deeds.

"My God, My God, why have You forsaken Me?" These words move us to such sorrow because we *do* know Who spoke them and because we do know Who hung bleeding and dying on that cross—not a mere man, not a fanatical rabbi, not an idealist who was caught up in the religious and political foment of His time; rather, Jesus Christ, God the Son, our Lord and Savior. The One who came to fulfill Scripture. The One in whom every promise of redemption was fulfilled.

## Unimaginable Suffering

When Jesus cried out, "My God, My God, why have You forsaken Me"—He was expressing the very depths of hell He experienced in atoning for our sins.

Admittedly, some disagree with this interpretation. They say that Jesus was simply quoting from Psalm 22:1, that Jesus may have *felt* forsaken by God, but that He was never *actually* forsaken by God. They insist that God the Father would never forsake God the Son, and especially not in the hour of His utmost suffering, pain, and need; furthermore, that God the Father would never forsake the Son of whom He twice testified: "This is My beloved Son, in whom I am well pleased," Matthew 3:17 and 17:5.

Yet, to think that the crucified Jesus was not forsaken by God the Father, that Jesus did not suffer hell for our sakes, is to forget the meaning of substitutionary atonement. It is to underestimate God's wrath against sin and to minimize what God the Father willingly sacrificed—and what God the Son willingly endured—to atone for all our sins.

On Good Friday, God the Father did utterly forsake the Son. Why? For the simple reason, as Paul explained in 2 Corinthians 5:21, "For He made Him who knew no sin to be sin for us, that we might become the righteousness of God in Him."

When the Father laid the iniquity of us all on His Son, He treated that only Son as if He were the world's only sinner. He rejected Him, turned away from Him, punished Him, so that He would not have to reject, forsake, and punish us.

"My God, My God, why have You forsaken Me?"

Jesus speaks. Do we hear him?

# Thirst

## John 19:28

*"After this, Jesus, knowing that all things were now accomplished, that the Scripture might be fulfilled, said, 'I thirst!'"*

It was past 3:00 P.M. on Good Friday. Jesus had now endured the cross for more than six hours, enduring not simply the physical torment of crucifixion—iron spikes in wrists and feet, dislocated bones, the constant struggle to breathe—but far worse, the divine punishment for the world's sin.

During these six hours, 9:00 A.M. to 3:00 P.M., Jesus had spoken four times. Once for the world: "Father, forgive them." Once to a penitent thief: "Today you will be with Me in Paradise." Once to His mother Mary and His disciple John: "Behold your son." "Behold your mother." And once more when He experienced utter abandonment by God the Father because of our sins: "My God, My God, why have You forsaken Me?"

Now, after 3:00 P.M., the dreadful darkness that had covered the land was giving way to afternoon sunshine and lengthening shadows. Between harsh curses and pagan prayers, the Roman soldiers doused their torches and resumed their grizzly tasks. Of the three men on the cross, the Man in the middle puzzled them most—the One with the superscription reading JESUS OF NAZARETH, KING OF THE JEWS. The One even Pilate pronounced innocent.

Then, with His death near and His redemptive work done, Jesus spoke a fifth time from the cross. His words were few and simple: "I thirst!" Of all four gospel writers, John alone, the same John who stood with Mary beneath the cross, recorded these words of Jesus.

"I thirst!" Upon first consideration, we may view this short sentence as relatively unimportant; at least, not as important as "Father, forgive" or "with Me in Paradise," and certainly not as important as "It is finished." Yet, the words "I thirst!" were not merely a pause between promise and fulfillment, between the pangs of hell and joys of victory. Every word Jesus spoke from the cross had meaning, purpose, and application, including the two words "I thirst!" Again we ask, What did these words mean to Jesus? What do they mean for us?

### Jesus Was Thirsty

Jesus said "I thirst!" because He *was* thirsty. Who wouldn't be after an ordeal like His? Hours of interrogation. Enormous blood loss from the beatings, scourging, crowning with thorns, and crucifixion. Forced to carry His own cross—likely the crossbeam or *patibulum*, which itself weighed from eighty to one hundred pounds—six hundred and fifty yards from Pilate's Praetorium to Golgotha, with most of the journey going uphill. And once at Golgotha, nailed to the cross, exposed to the elements, and panting and fighting for every breath for more than six hours.

And lest we forget, Jesus suffered all this while carrying the weight of the world's sin. Most of us know how heavy the guilt of even one sin can be. Imagine carrying the weight and guilt of every sin and every sinner. No wonder the Savior was sweating great drops of blood already in Gethsemane. Of course He was thirsty!

And throughout that entire ordeal, did anyone offer Jesus a drink? Ironically, the one time the Roman soldiers did offer Jesus a drink, that is, when preparing to drive iron spikes through His wrists and feet, He refused to take it. Do you know why? The drink was a mixture of wine and myrrh and meant to dull His pain. And no matter how thirsty Jesus was, this He would not allow. Rather, in accomplishing our eternal salvation, He atoned for every sin and experienced every pain to the uttermost.

## Jesus Was Human

Jesus also said "I thirst!" because He was truly human. He bled. He felt pain. He laughed and cried, hungered and thirsted, walked and talked, suffered and died. As Martin Luther wrote in his explanation of the Second Article in the Apostles' Creed: "I believe that Jesus Christ, true God begotten of the Father from eternity, and also true Man, born of the Virgin Mary, is my Lord."

And so, Jesus thirsted on the cross not only because of His suffering, but also because of His humanity. This is an important lesson. Haven't all of us at times doubted God's ability to relate to ordinary human problems? Instead, we wonder, "How can God understand what I'm going through? He's eternal; I'm mortal. He fills the universe; I live in a one-bedroom apartment. He's all-powerful; I'm weak. He's all-knowing; I'm confused. He's perfect; I'm sinful, flawed, wrinkled, bifocaled, and need a walker to cross the living room. How can He understand me?"

The answer to our doubt is that Jesus truly shared our humanity. He became as human as we are, yet was without sin. The apostle John wrote of Jesus, "And the Word became flesh and dwelt among us, and we beheld His glory, the glory as of the only begotten of the Father, full of grace and truth," John 1:14.

## Jesus Was Fulfilling Scripture

Consider again what John wrote in his gospel: "After this, Jesus, knowing that all things were now accomplished, that the Scripture might be fulfilled, said, 'I thirst!'" John 19:28. The Scriptures Jesus fulfilled with those two words were from the Book of Psalms. Psalm 22:15, "My strength is dried up like a potsherd, and My tongue clings to My jaws." Also Psalm 69:21, "They also gave me gall for My food, and for My thirst they gave Me vinegar to drink." Prophetic details about Christ's crucifixion that were given more than a thousand years before the Good Friday event.

But that is how faithful our God is. Faithful to each word, each promise, each detail, and each cross-reference. When others hung on the cross blaspheming God and cursing their executioners and proclaiming their innocence, Jesus Christ hung on the cross fulfilling Scripture with His final words and dying breaths.

## Jesus Was Our Substitute

I can't help but think that the words "I thirst!" meant more than physical thirst. Everything Jesus did on that cross He did as our perfect substitute. He died for our sins. He died for our place in Paradise. He died for our relationships. He died to suffer our hell. Is it not possible, then, that with the words "I thirst!" Jesus was also speaking as our substitute, that He was expressing the dreadful thirst that every human being has by nature, whether recognized or not?

The thirst for rest, purpose, and belonging. The thirst for something lasting and eternal. The thirst for something of which time cannot rob us and death cannot cheat us. In other words, the thirst for the living God.

Jesus spoke of this thirst in John 4, when He told a thirsting, searching Samaritan woman, "Whoever drinks of the water that I shall give him will never thirst." He said again in John 7, "If anyone thirsts, let him come to Me and drink. He who believes in Me, as the Scripture has said, out of his heart will flow rivers of living water." And He spoke of this thirst a final time when, on Good Friday, shortly before His atoning death for the world, He said, "I thirst!"

## Jesus Was Preparing

And then there is this: Jesus said "I thirst!" because He was about to say the most powerful, comforting, and life-changing words ever spoken. He wanted to wet His lips and parched throat a final time so that He could say the words loud enough for the world to hear them: "It is finished."

Jesus speaks. Do we hear Him?

# Finished

### John 19:30

*"So when Jesus had received the sour wine, He said, 'It is finished!' And bowing His head, He gave up His spirit."*

Maundy Thursday evening, the Garden of Gethsemane, where Jesus is betrayed with a kiss and arrested like a common criminal. Afterwards, He is interrogated for hours by Pilate the Prefect, Herod the King, and Caiaphas the High Priest. He is mocked, spit upon, beaten beyond recognition, dressed in royal purple, crowned with thorns, and scourged. "Here is the Man," Pilate shouts. It is meant to be a joke. It is meant to say, "Surely this Man is not worth the effort of crucifixion or the cost of the nails." But they all insist, "Crucify Him! Crucify Him!" So He is sentenced to death.

Good Friday, 9:00 A.M., on the stony hill of Golgotha. Jesus is nailed to the cross with iron spikes, then set between two reviling criminals. The pain is beyond description. He struggles to breathe. Yet, He still speaks words of forgiveness, acceptance, relationship, torment and utter abandonment, and thirst.

When He says, "I thirst," a Roman soldier soaks a sponge in sour wine-vinegar; places it on a stalk of the hyssop plant; and raises it to Jesus' lips. And it is here, with His bloody lips moistened and His parched throat wet, that Jesus speaks a sixth time. Beyond this, He will speak only once more. He says, "It is finished." Yet, remarkably, these words are not spoken in a loud voice. Instead, they are spoken as a clear, simple, unmistakable statement of divine fact. And as such, they are among the most important words of God ever spoken to lost mankind: "It is finished!"

Of course, on that dreadful Friday at Golgotha, the

adversaries of Jesus interpreted His words and death to mean that *He* was finished—the proof that He was nothing more than a Messianic pretender. Yet, little did they know that in God's redemptive plan, when all seemed lost, precisely then all was won. "It is finished!" was Christ's cry of victory, in perpetuity, of an irrevocably complete salvation.

"It is finished!" What was finished?

## Christ Finished His Suffering

Yes, we're aware of Christ's suffering. We read about it in in Scripture. We meditate on it every Lent. Yet, despite our familiarity with the Passion History, despite reading Bible passages like "then they spat in His face and beat Him," Matthew 26:67, despite knowing the pain of scourging and the agonies of crucifixion—the blood loss, the dislocated bones, the constant struggle to breathe, the shame of being crucified naked—you and I have no real understanding of what our Lord Jesus Christ suffered to redeem us. If we did understand, would we ever take sin lightly? Would we ever complain about our personal circumstances or anything we might suffer for the sake of Christ's name?

The fact is, the physical torture Jesus endured was not the worst of His suffering. The worst suffering came from carrying our every sin, every misdeed, every wrong thought, and every ill-spoken word. The worst suffering came from enduring our punishment because, as Isaiah wrote, "And the LORD has laid on Him the iniquity of us all," Isaiah 53:6.

## Christ Finished His Work

Christ's suffering ended when His work was done, when everything was paid for and everything was suffered. So we read of Jesus in John 19:28, "After this, Jesus, knowing that *all things were now accomplished. . .*"

With His work done and salvation won, Jesus said, "It is finished!" While there are three words in English, there is only one word in Greek: *TETELESTAI*; a word with a glorious meaning. The basic meaning of *TETELESTAI* is "to finish, complete, fulfill, bring to an end." Yet, when the apostle John, writing under inspiration of the Holy Spirit, used the word *TETELESTAI* for "it is finished," he placed it in a special verb tense—what Greek grammarians call the Perfect Tense. This tense views an action as completed and having abiding results, that is, ongoing blessings. What was the completed action? Christ's death on the cross. What are the abiding results of Christ's death? Forgiveness and salvation for all who trust in Jesus as Lord and Savior.

Consider carefully what this means. It means that no matter who you are, no matter what you've done, no matter when you've lived—whether you've believed in Christ since infancy, as did Timothy; or whether you came to faith in Christ during the last hours of your life, as did the penitent thief on the cross—the who, what, or when simply don't matter. In Jesus Christ you have a PERFECTLY COMPLETE salvation. Done. Won. Accomplished. Finished. And yours through faith.

"It is finished!" At the time of Jesus, that Greek word *TETELESTAI* was commonly used in seaports, marketplaces, customs seats, and various other government sites for financial transactions. Archaeologists have found thousands of ancient business documents inscribed with the same word that was used in John 19:30. Why? Because *TETELESTAI* meant PAID IN FULL. And that Scripture incorporated this commonplace financial term in describing the words of Jesus—"It is finished!"—leaves no doubt as to their meaning. Jesus was declaring, "I have paid your debt in full. Nothing is missing. Nothing is undone. Nothing is incomplete."

Our Bible is the receipt of that paid-in-full salvation. When we look at the failures, weaknesses, and sins in our lives; when we cry out with Paul, "What a wretched person I am. Who will rescue me from this body of death?"—we can answer with Paul, "Thanks be to God, through Jesus Christ our Lord!" We can say, "Here is my receipt. This Bible. These words of Jesus Christ, which declare that the debt of all my sins has been PAID IN FULL."

## Christ Finished God's Promises of Redemption

Somewhere I read that more than three hundred and fifty Old Testament prophecies were fulfilled in the coming of Jesus Christ. And many of them had to do with Christ's once-for-all sacrifice to atone for the world's sin.

The Passion History repeatedly states "this happened so that the Scripture would be fulfilled." That Jesus would be betrayed for thirty pieces of silver. That all of His disciples would forsake Him and flee. That He would be beaten beyond recognition. That He would be scourged, then crucified alongside of two malefactors.

Even in Gethsemane, Jesus told His disciples, "Or do you think that I cannot now pray to My Father, and He will provide Me with more than twelve legions of angels? How then could the Scriptures be fulfilled, that it must happen thus?" Matthew 26:53-54.

Indeed, as Jesus hung dying on the cross, He was still fulfilling Scripture. When He cried out, "My God, My God, why have You forsaken Me?" He was fulfilling Psalm 22:1. When He cried out, "I thirst!" He was fulfilling Psalm 22:15 and Psalm 69:21. And when He cried out, "It is finished" He was fulfilling every promise God ever made about providing our eternal salvation.

As you see Jesus on that cross, His head bowed and crowned with thorns, His precious blood dripping to the ground; as you hear Him fulfill Scripture to the last word, with His last breath, know with certainty that the God on that cross, your God, is the God Who keeps His promises.

"It is finished."

Jesus speaks. Do we hear Him?

# Death

Luke 23:46

*"And when Jesus had cried out with a loud voice, He said, 'Father, into Your hands I commit My spirit.' Having said this, He breathed His last."*

The Passion History of Jesus Christ is recorded in all four gospels: Matthew, Mark, Luke, and John. Reading this history, some may conclude that Jesus was more a victim of circumstances than controlling them.

He was arrested in Gethsemane, paraded before Caiaphas and Pilate and Herod, bound, beaten, bloodied, dressed in royal purple, and crowned with thorns. And He was relentlessly mocked. "Prophesy to us, Christ!" jeered the soldiers. "Who is the one who struck You?" Matthew 26:68. Even as Jesus hung on the cross, passersby shook their heads and wagged their tongues, saying, "If You are the Son of God, come down from the cross," Matthew 27:40.

Envision the scenes: Jesus, silent before His lying accusers. Jesus, less desirable to the frenzied mobs than the cold-hearted killer Barabbas. Jesus, condemned though innocent, crucified though God.

And yet, that which happened to our Savior throughout His passion was not by accident, but by God's eternal design. Though the nations raged and peoples plotted and rulers schemed against the Lord and His anointed Christ—clearly prophesied in Psalm 2—the living, reigning God merely used their arrogance to accomplish His purposes.

Even before the events of Passion Week, Jesus told the Jews, "Therefore My Father loves Me, because I lay down My life that I may take it again. *No one takes it from Me, but I lay it down of Myself.* I have power to lay it down, and I have power to take it again. This command I have received from

My Father," John 10:17-18.

That Jesus was in complete control of His passion, including the time and means of His death, is evident even from His final words on the cross: "And when Jesus had cried out with a loud voice, He said, 'Father, into Your hands I commit My spirit,'" Luke 23:46. "I commit," He said. The Greek word used literally means "I place alongside" or "I entrust to." With His work done and our salvation won, Jesus offered up His life.

But this we seldom consider: With His final words on the cross, Jesus also taught us to face our own death with absolute confidence and joyful hope in our heavenly Father.

Death is not a happy topic. Some years ago, while pastoring a congregation, I also worked as a Family Services Advisor at a Florida funeral home. Part of my responsibilities included selling pre-need funeral arrangements. I quickly learned that though "planning ahead" provided many advantages—cost savings, financing, removing the burden of planning from grieving loved ones—still, the vast majority of people refused to even contemplate their death, much less plan for it.

None of us *want* to die. None of us were meant to die. God created Adam and Eve to live fully and eternally, not to plan funerals and mourn the loss of loved ones. Death came into the world through sin, as Paul explained in Romans 5: "Therefore, just as through one man sin entered the world, and death through sin, and thus death spread to all men, because all sinned."

To think that Jesus relished the prospect of death, especially death on a cross, is to overlook His humanity and the prayer He prayed while face down in Gethsemane, amid tears and groans: "O My Father, if it is possible, let this cup pass from Me," Matthew 26:39.

Yet, neither did Jesus fear death. He knew well the necessity of His death for the life of Mankind, and He spoke of it often to His disciples. In Matthew 16:21, for example, we're told that "from that time Jesus began to show to His disciples that He *must* go to Jerusalem, and suffer many things from the elders and chief priests and scribes, and be killed, and be raised the third day."

### The Heavenly Father

Jesus faced His death as He lived His life: with complete, unshakable trust in His Father in heaven. Indeed, He spoke of this relationship often during His ministry; from His words as a twelve-year-old in the temple, "Did you not know that I must be about My Father's business?" Luke 2:49; to His last words and last breath on the cross, "Father, into Your hands I commit My spirit," Luke 23:46.

Through Jesus Christ, this same Father in heaven is now *our* heavenly Father. A fact Jesus emphasized multiple times in His Sermon on the Mount. A fact He stated when teaching us how to pray: "Our Father who art in heaven." And a fact He stated again shortly after His resurrection, saying, "I am ascending to My Father and *your* Father, and to My God and your God," John 20:17.

"Father, into Your hands. . . ." Jesus said these words not only as our perfect Savior and perfect Substitute, but also as our perfect Example. At the moment of our death, we do not pass into the unknown, but to the Father we've known all our lives through Jesus Christ, the Father Who chose us to be His own before time began and loved us enough to sacrifice His only Son for our sins. *That* Father. *His* outstretched, waiting arms. As Christians, we know where we go at death, but even more importantly, we know to WHOM we go at death. Our *ABBA*, the Aramaic word Jesus would have used when He said, "Father, into Your hands." A term of implicit trust and endearment.

### A Bedtime Prayer

When Jesus said, "Father, into Your hands I commit My spirit," He was not only praying, He was reciting and fulfilling

Scripture. The words are from Psalm 31:5, which Jesus personalized by prefacing the verse with "Father." The psalm verse reads, "Into Your hand I commit my spirit; You have redeemed me, O LORD God of truth." The word of God that Jesus lived, breathed, and taught in life was the very same word that sustained Him in the hour of death. Surely, the same is true of us.

But there is even more significance to these final words of the Savior. At the time of Jesus, Psalm 31:5 was taught to Jewish children as a bedtime prayer, similar to our "Now I lay me down to sleep" or the prayer my grandparents used to say at bedtime: "Now the light has gone away; Father listen while I pray, asking Thee to watch and keep and to send me quiet sleep."

Jesus closed His eyes in death the way He once, as a child, closed them in sleep—with a simple, childlike prayer in which He asked His Father to watch over Him. A beautiful picture. With His redemptive work done, Jesus offered up His life. And because of the redemption Jesus obtained for us on that bloody cross, we too can "fall asleep" in the Lord, knowing our salvation is certain, knowing our heavenly Father is waiting, and knowing, as Jesus did, that beyond our death lies our glorious resurrection.

The author of Hebrews wrote of Jesus, "Inasmuch then as the children have partaken of flesh and blood, He Himself likewise shared in the same, that through death He might destroy him who had the power of death, that is, the devil, and release those who through fear of death were all their lifetime subject to bondage," Hebrews 2:14-15.

In the words of the hymnist: "It is not death to die, to leave this weary road, and midst the brotherhood on high to be at home with God."

"Father, into Your hands I commit My spirit." Jesus speaks. Do we hear Him?

# Seven Petitions

# The Lord's Prayer

Luke 11:1

*When God's people pray, He is "all ears." He listens so closely, so carefully, that He knows our petitions before we present them.*

Jesus was praying. Afterwards, one disciple approached Him and asked, "Lord, teach us to pray." But what prompted this request? Surely, the disciples knew how to pray. They were Jewish men from Jewish households. They attended temple worship services, heard the priests, and recited psalms. And yet, when they witnessed Jesus pray, they must have seen a frequency, vibrancy, and intimacy missing from their own prayer life.

Jesus prayed often. He prayed during the momentous occasions of His life and ministry: His baptism and transfiguration, when He fed the five thousand and raised Lazarus from the dead, in the Garden of Gethsemane and on the mount called Calvary. "Father, forgive them" and "Father, into Your hands" were both prayers.

But Jesus also prayed amid daily circumstances: before sleeping, after waking, when filled with joy at His Father's wisdom and grace. "I thank You, Father," He prayed, "Lord of heaven and earth, that You have hidden these things from the wise and prudent and have revealed them to babes," Matthew 11:25. Indeed, prayer was such an integral part of Christ's life that He often withdrew from the crowds to pray, as stated in Luke 5:16, "He Himself often withdrew into the wilderness and prayed."

Yet, Jesus not only exemplified prayer, He frequently taught about prayer. He taught that prayer is powerful and effective, that prayers should be offered in humility yet with persistence, but not with mindless repetition. "And when you pray," He said, "do not use vain repetitions as the heathen do. For they think that they will be heard for their many words," Matthew 6:7.

"Lord, teach us to pray." Surely, this is a fitting request for us to ask, too. Like the first disciples, we are familiar with prayer. We pray on various occasions, in many locations and at many times: home, church, work, at meals, before bed, and certainly in times of distress and trouble.

Yet, have we nothing to learn about prayer? Is our prayer life as vibrant, frequent, and intimate as it should be? Don't we, at times, have misconceptions about prayer? "God won't hear my prayers unless they are eloquently spoken and grammatically correct." Or, "God is too busy to answer my prayers." Or, "God pays more attention to the prayers of the clergy than the laity." Such views are wrong.

Ultimately, prayer is simply talking with God. And it doesn't matter if the prayers are polished and formal or halting and stumbling. The Holy Spirit can translate even sobs, sighs, and groans into the most eloquent of prayers, heard and acted upon by the Almighty.

When God's people pray, He is "all ears." He listens so closely that He knows our petitions *before* we present them. He Himself has invited us to pray, saying, "Ask, and it will be given to you; seek, and you will find; knock, and it will be opened to you," Matthew 7:7. The verb tenses used in this verse are all in the present tense—literally, "go on asking," "go on seeking," "go on knocking." Does this sound as if God is not interested in our prayers?

Jesus did teach His disciples how to pray, using the familiar and cherished words of the Lord's Prayer. This prayer is remarkable not only for its wording, but also for its structure. With the introduction, "Our Father who art in heaven," Jesus taught us HOW to pray; that is, we are to approach God with confidence, knowing that He is our heavenly Father through the atoning sacrifice of Christ.

In the seven petitions—from "Hallowed be Thy name" to

"Deliver us from evil"—Jesus exemplified WHAT to pray. The first three petitions focus on God: His name, His kingdom, and His will. The last four petitions focus on us: our daily bread, our forgiveness, our protection, and our deliverance.

And finally, in the conclusion, Jesus reminded us WHY we pray to the one true God: "For Thine is the kingdom and the power and the glory forever and ever. Amen." God alone is the source of all grace, power, and blessings. And this God hears and answers our prayers.

Consequently, even with the structure of the Lord's Prayer, Jesus taught valuable lessons about praying. We are to approach God in confidence. We are to present our needs and wants. We are to depart in peace, knowing that God will hear and answer in His time and in His way.

The apostle Paul offered the very same advice on prayer in Philippians 4:6-7. He said, "Be anxious for nothing, but in everything by prayer and supplication, with thanksgiving, let your requests be made known to God; and the peace of God, which surpasses all understanding, will guard your hearts and minds through Christ Jesus."

Approach. Pray. Depart in peace.

# Our Father Who Art in Heaven

## Luke 11:2

*Everything about prayer, from the way we approach God to what we expect from God, is predicated on one wondrous relationship: "Our Father who art in heaven."*

When teaching His disciples how to pray, Jesus said first, "When you pray, say: 'Our Father in heaven,'" Luke 11:2. Why would the Savior emphasize this relationship before teaching His disciples to pray for daily sustenance, forgiveness, protection, and deliverance from evil?

The answer is simple and important. Everything about prayer, from how we approach God to what we expect from God, is based on this blessed relationship; namely, that God *the* Father is now God *our* Father through the atoning sacrifice of Christ and the sanctifying work of the Holy Spirit. God is our God. We are God's people. Jesus pointedly said after His resurrection, "I am ascending to My Father and *your* Father, and to My God and *your* God," John 20:17.

Jesus viewed this Father-child relationship as so important to a Christian's life, behavior, confidence, and prayer that He used the phrase "your Father in heaven" no less than twelve times in His Sermon on the Mount.

Martin Luther, who once thought of God the Father only as a dreadful, vengeful Judge, wrote the following after coming to understand the gospel—after coming to see God the Father through the sacrifice of God the Son: "God would by these words tenderly invite us to believe that He is our true Father, that we are His true children, so that we may with all boldness and confidence ask Him as dear children ask their dear father."

## Approaching in Confidence

Paul wrote in Romans 8, "For you did not receive the spirit of bondage again to fear, but you received the Spirit of adoption by whom we cry out, 'Abba, Father.'" *ABBA* is an Aramaic word; and its meaning resembles its sound. *ABBA*. Da-da. Dad. A term of endearment. A term that evokes images of a toddler leaping joyfully into his father's arms; no fear, only trust and a mutual embrace.

This is the picture Jesus painted for us with the words "our Father who art in heaven." A picture of confidence, trust, joy; of a heavenly Father Who wants us in His arms as much as we want to be there.

God richly blessed me with a wonderful Christian father, who loved me, protected and provided for me, encouraged and disciplined me, and picked me up when I fell—literally and figuratively. To the day of my father's death, I knew I could approach him with any problem. Even when breathing through a respirator, he still insisted on telling me, "I love you," and as I was leaving his hospital room, "Be sure to drive safely, son." That was my father. Always thinking of others. Seldom thinking of himself. And if this is true of an earthly father, how much truer must it be of our perfect Father in heaven.

When we think, "Prayer is of no use; God isn't listening to me"—this is not viewing God as our loving Father but as a complete stranger, as the Father we've never seen and therefore don't know. But we have seen Him and we do know Him through the coming of our Lord Jesus Christ.

As Jesus told Philip, "Have I been with you so long, and yet you have not known Me, Philip? He who has seen Me has seen the Father," John 14:9. It is in the coming, dying, and rising of Jesus Christ that we also see the great love of God the Father. And if the Father was willing to sacrifice His Son for us, why would we imagine Him as unwilling to hear our prayers?

## Praying in Humility

Jesus once told a parable about a Pharisee and a tax collector who went into the temple to pray. The Pharisee stood in a prominent place, boasting about his goodness and accomplishments.

By contrast, the tax collector stood at a distance, cloaked in shadow. Unable to lift his eyes heavenward, he struck his chest—a sign of guilt, grief, and remorse—and offered a short, humble prayer: "God, be merciful to me a sinner," Luke 18:13.

Which of these two prayers did God choose to hear? The Pharisee's words were not a prayer but an arrogant boast: "Because I do such great things for you, God; You, God, are obligated to do great things for me." The tax collector, however, prayed in humility because he recognized his sin and unworthiness.

When you and I pray "Our Father who art in heaven," we are praying in view of a relationship that we did not earn and do not deserve. That God would, as Martin Luther stated, "tenderly invite us to believe that He is our true Father and that we are His true children," should move each of us to pray with humility and gratitude; and to proclaim with the apostle John, "Behold what manner of love the Father has bestowed on us, that we should be called children of God,"1 John 3:1.

## Praying in Hopeful Expectation

When we pray, we should always expect the best from God. Why? Because God *is* our loving Father in heaven. And unlike us, He never confuses our wants with our needs. He never allows our earthly desires to interfere with His heavenly designs to save us. The gifts God gives are always good and perfect gifts, as the apostle James wrote, "Every good gift and every perfect gift is from above, and comes down from the Father of lights, with whom there is no variation or shadow of turning," James 1:17.

And so Jesus taught His disciples, "Or what man is there

among you who, if his son asks for bread, will give him a stone? Or if he asks for a fish, will he give him a serpent? If you then, being evil, know how to give good gifts to your children, how much more will your Father who is in heaven give good things to those who ask Him!" Matthew 7:9-11.

Jesus taught us to pray in view of a wondrous relationship: God is our Father. Truthfully, doesn't that make you want to leap into His arms and feel His embrace through Scripture? Doesn't that make you want to sit in His lap and entrust all of your good times and bad, successes and failures, problems and worries, to His keeping?

Our Father's welcome mat is always out. Jesus is the one who said, "Ask, and it will be given to you; seek, and you will find; knock, and it will be opened to you," Matthew 7:7.

So ask, seek, and knock. Your heavenly Father is listening and waiting to answer.

# Hallowed be Thy Name

Luke 11:2

*With only little reflection, we can see how wrong it is to take the very names of God that speak of His love, salvation, and divine nature; and then use them to condemn, curse, or jest.*

The word *hallowed* is seldom used in modern English. In fact, its principal use may be in the Lord's Prayer, along with a seasonal reference to Halloween—which is a contraction of *hallowed* and *evening*. The basic meaning of *hallowed* is "holy." The Greek word translated as "hallowed" in the Lord's Prayer, *HAGIAZO*, has the sense of pure, clean, consecrated, called and set apart for sacred use.

Similarly, the Greek word for *saint* in the New Testament, *HAGIOS*, refers to one who is set apart by God and for God; that is, a believer in Jesus Christ, and therefore one who is washed clean in the blood of Christ. As John wrote in his First Epistle: "The blood of Jesus Christ His Son cleanses us from all sin," 1 John 1:7.

But what are we asking God when we pray, "Hallowed be Thy name"? What are God's names, and what do His names teach us?

## God's Names

Scripture contains many names for God, and each one describes some characteristic of His divine nature. To be clear, these are not names we chose for God, but names by which God revealed Himself to us—names often suited to specific circumstances.

For example, the name *ELOHIM*, first used in Genesis 1:1, describes the majestic God of creation. *ELOHIM* is actually a plural name, not in the sense of "many gods," but in the sense of abundance and plurality of attributes. God is the *all*-powerful and *all*-wise God, as He would have to be to create all things from no things.

When God promised Abraham a son, the patriarch was already old and reproductively dead. His wife Sarah was also elderly and barren. In this context of human impossibility, God revealed Himself by the name of *EL SHADDAI*; a name meaning "God Almighty." He is the God for Whom nothing is impossible. "Is anything too hard for the LORD?" He asked Abraham. And make no mistake, in our impossible circumstances, *EL SHADDAI* asks the same of us.

When Moses felt overwhelmed by his call to lead the Israelites out of Egypt, God revealed Himself by the name of *YAVEH* or *Jehovah*; a Hebrew verb meaning "I AM," and perhaps the one name for God more than any other that emphasizes His eternal nature and covenant faithfulness.

At its simplest, *eternal* means "always there." And this is reflected in that great name "I AM." With His very name, God is saying, "I AM with you always. I AM with you in your youth and age. I AM with you in your joy and sorrow, health and sickness, wealth and poverty, time and eternity."

Or consider the many names and titles of Jesus in the New Testament. *Jesus* means "Savior." *Christ* means "the Anointed One". Hence, Jesus Christ is the one and only Savior. This great truth is reflected in other names Jesus applied to Himself: the Way, the Truth, the Life, the Gate, the Vine, the Bread of Life, the Good Shepherd, and the Resurrection.

Then, that heartwarming name and title of the Holy Spirit: the Comforter. The Greek word is *PARAKLATOS*, and it literally means *to call to the side of*. The picture is that of a mother sweeping her hurting child into her arms and saying, "Don't worry. Everything will be all right." This the Holy Spirit does by leading us into the arms of Jesus Christ through the gospel.

And there are scores of other names for God in the Bible; each precious, each holy, each given by God Himself to help us know Him better, and each to be "hallowed"; that is, treasured, held in esteem, used properly, and treated with reverential awe and respect—in much the same way that God told Moses at the burning bush, "Take your sandals off your feet, for the place where you stand is holy ground," Exodus 3:5.

With only little reflection, we can see how wrong it is to take the very names of God that speak of His divine nature, love, presence, faithfulness, and salvation; and then use them to condemn, curse, or jest. No matter what the circumstances, mindlessly spouting "Jesus Christ" or "Oh, my God" cannot be construed as hallowing God's name.

Oh, how zealously we protect our own names; wincing at mispronunciations, correcting misspellings, refusing to let "our good names" be raked through the mud of gossip and false testimony. But what of God's good names? Does He care how His names are used? Actually, He speaks clearly on the matter in Exodus 20:7, and His words are very sobering: "You shall not take the name of the LORD your God in vain, for the LORD will not hold him guiltless who takes His name in vain."

## God's Word

Names describe. While God's personal names and titles describe Him, so does His holy Word—and to a far, far greater extent. In the name *EL SHADDAI*, we witness the almighty power of God; in *YAVEH*, the eternity of God; in *Jesus*, the Savior of Mankind; in *PARAKLATOS*, the comforting work of the Holy Spirit. All of these personal names describe some aspect of God's divine nature.

But in His Word, God gives us the fullest revelation of who He is, what He is like, and what He has done. He reveals His Triunity; the origin of the universe; the fall into sin; the utter depravity of sinful human nature; the first promise of the Savior; redemptive history carried out from Adam, through

Abraham and the Patriarchs, through the nation of Israel; to the birth, ministry, suffering, death, and resurrection of the World's Only Savior, Jesus Christ; and the glorious inheritance awaiting all those who trust in Him.

In His Word God reveals what cannot be revealed in a single name or title—especially the way for lost Mankind to be saved. As Paul wrote: "from childhood you have known the Holy Scriptures, which are able to make you wise for salvation through faith which is in Christ Jesus. All Scripture is given by inspiration of God, and is profitable for doctrine, for reproof, for correction, for instruction in righteousness, that the man of God may be complete, thoroughly equipped for every good work," 2 Timothy 3:15-17.

To hallow God's name, then, also means to hallow God's Word, to treat it with reverence, to accept its authority, to take from it and not read into it, to recognize every word as God's word, to stand on its every teaching with heads bowed and sandals off, knowing—as Moses did at the burning bush—that we are standing on HALLOWED ground, and to tremble at God's Word in the way that He spoke of in Isaiah 66:2: "But on this one will I look: On him who is poor and of a contrite spirit, and who trembles at My word."

Such is to hallow the name of God. And in the First Petition, this is what we're asking God to enable us to do.

As with all the petitions of the Lord's Prayer, Martin Luther's explanation of the First Petition, "Hallowed be Thy name," is simple and succinct. He wrote, "God's name is indeed holy in itself; but we pray in this petition that it may be holy among us also." God's name is hallowed "when the word of God is taught in its truth and purity, and we, as the children of God, also lead a holy life according to it. This grant us, dear Father in heaven. But he that teaches and lives otherwise than God's word teaches, profanes the name of God among us. From this preserve us, heavenly Father."

# Thy Kingdom Come

## Luke 11:2

*A kingdom is that which is ruled by a king. The kingdom of God is His gracious rule in human hearts.*

"Thy kingdom come." Familiar words spoken countless times since Jesus taught them to His disciples. But what do the words mean? What are we praying for? What is the kingdom of God?

A kingdom is that which is ruled by a king, his dominion. In one sense, the universe is God's kingdom because it is *His* universe. He made it. He has complete dominion over it and everything in it: every person, every place, every nation, every circumstance. The psalmist wrote, "The LORD has established His throne in heaven, and His kingdom rules over all," Psalm 103:19.

Regardless of what we read in the daily newspaper or watch on the nightly news; terrorists, politicians, economies, and worldly governments are not controlling our lives. God is. God has never abdicated His throne and never will.

Therefore, this type of kingdom—that is, the fact of God's absolute sovereignty over His universe—is not something we need to pray for. It exists. Instead, our prayer should be, "Lord, amid all the chaos and craziness of this world, help me to see that You are in absolute control; that nothing can happen without Your direction or permission."

When Jesus taught us to pray, "Thy kingdom come," He was talking about another kind of kingdom; specifically, the gracious rule of God in the human heart, a rule that begins when the Holy Spirit brings a dead, darkened human heart to life and faith in Jesus Christ.

This kingdom is not visible, material, or external. It has no boundary lines, no roads and bridges, no soldiers and armaments, no national currency or gross domestic product, no brick-and-mortar palace or jewel-encrusted throne. Countless Jews expected such a materialistic kingdom from their Messiah. And when Jesus rejected this carnal view of God's kingdom, many Jews rejected Him.

Yet, who is better qualified to define the nature of God's kingdom than its King? The phrases "kingdom of God" and "kingdom of heaven" are used more than one hundred times in the New Testament. And the majority of these references were made by Jesus Himself.

Jesus told Pilate, "My kingdom is not of this world," John 18:36. He told the Pharisees, "The kingdom of God does not come with observation; nor will they say, 'See here!' or 'See there!' For indeed, the kingdom of God is within you," Luke 17:20-21. And echoing Christ's teaching, Paul wrote in Romans 14:17, "For the kingdom of God is not eating and drinking, but righteousness and peace and joy in the Holy Spirit."

This is that blessed kingdom, God's gracious rule in the hearts of men, about which Jesus taught us to pray, "Thy kingdom come." This kingdom, as Luther rightly explained in his *Small Catechism*, "comes indeed without our prayer, of itself; but we pray in this petition that it may come unto us also."

But if God's kingdom comes without our prayer, why pray? In fact, if God knows our thoughts before we think them, and our words before we say them, why pray at all? Frequently asked questions with scripturally-based answers.

First, we pray because the Bible tells us to pray. And as Christians, we don't need another reason, do we? Second, we pray because Jesus saw prayer as important, powerful, and effective; and therefore we should, too. Remember, it was His prayer-life that led to the request, "Lord, teach us to pray."

Third, prayer is for our benefit, not God's.

Communication is important to any relationship, *especially* our relationship with God. It keeps us focused on God, reminds us of our dependence on Him, and brings us peace of heart and mind.

Fourth, we pray because God has promised to hear, answer, and act on every prayer of every believer. Fifth, we pray because, even though God knows what He will do, we don't. Lastly, we pray because prayer is more than asking. It also includes PRAISING God for the things He has done, is doing, and will continue to do.

### A Prayer for Ourselves

When we pray "Thy kingdom come," we are first of all praying that our gracious Father in heaven would rule powerfully and constantly in our own hearts. Martin Luther wrote in one of his Christmas hymns, "Ah, dearest Jesus, holy Child, make Thee a bed, soft, undefiled, within my heart that it may be a quiet chamber kept for Thee."

That God's kingdom has come to us should compel us to our knees in joy, humility, and thanksgiving—knowing that we had no part in entering it. As Paul wrote of God the Father: "He has delivered us from the power of darkness and conveyed us into the kingdom of the Son of His love," Colossians 1:13. Or as Jesus told His disciples in Luke 12:32, "Do not fear, little flock, for it is your Father's good pleasure to give you the kingdom."

With every day, every circumstance, every task, every relationship, every worry, every ache and pain, every Bible study, every breath, every heartbeat; in everything and every way we have reason to pray, "Thy kingdom come." With this simple petition, we are asking our heavenly Father to reign supreme in our lives, hearts, relationships, and priorities.

### A Prayer for Others

When we pray, "Thy kingdom come," we are also praying for other people: family, friends, neighbors, community, country, and ultimately our world. We're asking God to graciously extend His kingdom and lead others to faith and salvation in Christ. How does this happen? Only through the proclamation of the gospel. This is why Jesus placed such emphasis on sharing the good news of His kingdom; and why we read of Jesus Himself: "Then Jesus went about all the cities and villages, teaching in their synagogues, preaching the gospel of the kingdom, and healing every sickness and every disease among the people," Matthew 9:35.

Martin Luther explained the Second Petition of the Lord's Prayer this way: "God's kingdom certainly comes all by itself, even without our prayer, but we pray in this petition that it also come to us." *How does the kingdom of God come?* God's kingdom comes "when our heavenly Father gives us His Spirit, so that by His grace we believe His holy word and live a godly life here in time and hereafter in eternity."

## A Prayer for the Return of Our Savior

Finally, when we pray, "Thy kingdom come," we are also praying for the return of our Savior and the glorious consummation of His eternal kingdom, a kingdom only glimpsed in the pages of Scripture, a kingdom in which we will celebrate eternally with our God.

The next time you feel alone, unnoticed, unwanted, or unimportant, remember these words of Jesus—words that King Jesus will say to you when He returns at the end of the age: "Come, you blessed of My Father, inherit the kingdom prepared for you from the foundation of the world," Matthew 25:34.

Even so, come Lord Jesus.

# Thy Will Be Done

Luke 11:2

*We pray "Thy will be done," so that what is done without us might also be done within us.*

God's will is that which He decrees or desires. Yet surely, this will, *His* will, is done without our prayer and certainly without our permission. The psalmist wrote, "But our God is in heaven; He does whatever He pleases," Psalm 115:3. This being true, why did Jesus teach us to pray "Thy will be done"? What are we asking God for?

## Thy Will be Done in Our World

When we pray, "Thy will be done," we are asking God to overthrow every evil counsel or will that opposes His Christ, His Church, His Gospel, and especially His good and gracious desire that "all be saved and come to the knowledge of the truth," 1 Timothy 2:4. In Luther's words, God's will is done among us "when God breaks and hinders every evil counsel and will which would not let us hallow God's name nor let His kingdom come, such as the will of the devil, the world, and our flesh."

Hostile wills opposed the Christian Church from its beginning: jealous Judaizers and Roman emperors like Nero, who tossed Christians to starved lions and burned them as torches to illuminate his evening dinner parties. "Now, Lord," believers prayed, "look on their threats, and grant to Your servants that with all boldness they may speak Your word," Acts 4:29. In other words, "Thy will be done on earth as it is in heaven."

And God's will was done; yes, in answer to their prayers, but more importantly, in answer to God's eternal plans and purposes. This, too, the early Christians understood, that—though nations raged, peoples plotted, and kings stood defiantly against the Lord and His anointed Christ—when these God-opposers and Messiah-killers nailed Jesus to the cross, they were unwittingly carrying out God's eternal plan for mankind's redemption. They had not thwarted God's will. He had overthrown theirs.

In this the first Christians rejoiced, praising God and saying, "For truly against Your holy Servant Jesus, whom You anointed, both Herod and Pontius Pilate, with the Gentiles and the people of Israel, were gathered together to do whatever *Your hand and Your purpose determined before to be done*," Acts 4:27-28.

"Thy will be done on earth as it is in heaven." This is an important prayer for us, too—namely, that God would overthrow all those who hinder the hallowing of His name or the coming of His kingdom. For we live in an age of widespread, hellish opposition to Christianity. In fact, Christianity is the most persecuted religion on Earth today.

In 2016 alone, more than 90,000 Christians were murdered for the sake of Christ[1]—nearly one-third of those killed by Islamic terrorists. Christians may no longer be tossed to lions. But in countries like North Korea, they are starved, beaten, imprisoned, trampled, forced to have abortions, hung on crosses over fire, and even crushed by steamrollers.[2]

Even in our beloved United States, Christianity is increasingly under attack by atheists, secular progressives, politicians, and government legislation. Right is called wrong. Wrong is called right. And in addition to these "external" attacks, Christians also face "internal" conflicts and temptations that hinder God's will. There are the glittering allurements of the world, the ravenous appetite of Satan to

---

[1] FoxNews.com, *Christians the most persecuted group in the world for second straight year: Study*; by Perry Chiaramonte; January 6, 2017.
[2] Christianpost.com, *Christians 'Crushed Under Steamroller' and 'Hung on a Cross Over Fire' in North Korea*; by Samuel Smith; September 27, 2016.

lead us astray, and the Old Sinful Nature and its constant inclination to war against all that is good and godly.

Martin Luther wrote the following in one of his Reformation hymns: "Lord, keep us steadfast in Thy Word; curb those who fain by craft and sword would wrest the Kingdom from Thy Son and set at naught all He hath done." Aren't these words saying "Thy will be done on earth as it is in heaven"?

But let us also remember that in praying "Thy will be done," we are not simply praying for the overthrow of worldly opposition, but also for the world's salvation. Paul told Timothy, "Therefore I exhort first of all that supplications, prayers, intercessions, and giving of thanks be made for all men, for kings and all who are in authority, that we may lead a quiet and peaceable life in all godliness and reverence. For this is good and acceptable in the sight of God our Savior, *who desires all men to be saved and to come to the knowledge of the truth*," 1 Timothy 2:1-4.

When God breaks and hinders worldly opposition to His Word and our sharing of it, His gospel is proclaimed, His name is hallowed, His kingdom comes, and His salvation is received.

## Thy Will be Done in Our Lives

When we pray "Thy will be done," we are also praying that God's will be done in our lives, and that our will be conformed to His will. As Paul wrote in Romans 12:2, "And do not be conformed to this world, but be transformed by the renewing of your mind, that you may prove what is that good and acceptable and perfect will of God."

As Christians, we strive to serve and please God. Yet, at times, our wills can also be opposed to God's will through ignorance, misunderstanding, disobedience, or the mistaken belief that we know more than the All-Knowing God or that our will is more important than His will. It isn't. Living outside the will of God never brings happiness, only harm. So here, too, we pray "Thy will be done," asking that our heavenly Father topple our own will and plans if they interfere with His will and plans for our lives and salvation. To quote Solomon: "There are many plans in a man's heart, nevertheless the LORD'S counsel—that will stand," Proverbs 19:21.

Finally, when we pray "Thy will be done on earth as it is in heaven," we are also asking God to make His will known to us and to give us the strength and wisdom to do His will.

Where does God reveal His will to us—tell us how to be saved through faith in Christ; tell us how to live because of Christ; tell us how to think, speak, and act; how to prioritize, serve, love, forgive, respond to injustice, react to false teaching, treat our spouses, raise our children, face our death? God reveals His will in His Word—the Word that is from God and is inspired by God and therefore, as Paul wrote to Timothy, is able to "make you wise for salvation through faith in Christ Jesus" and also "thoroughly equipped for every good work," 2 Timothy 3:15, 17.

And the same Lord Who reveals His will to us will also empower us to do His will. This, too, is the promise of Scripture: "For it is God who works in you both to will and to do for His good pleasure," Philippians 2:13.

"Thy will be done on earth as it is in heaven." Or in the words of the hymnist,

Thy way, not mine, O Lord,
However dark it be.
Lead me by Thine own hand;
Choose Thou the path for me.
I dare not choose my lot;
I would not if I might.
Choose Thou for me, my God;
So shall I walk aright.

# Give Us This Day Our Daily Bread

## Luke 11:3

*By "daily bread," Jesus meant everything that we need to live on a daily basis. And where do these blessings come from? God.*

Jesus taught us to pray, "Give us this day our daily bread." But what did He mean by bread? And why the emphasis on daily?

### More Than Bread

When I was a boy, the words "give us this day our daily bread" always reminded me of a loaf of *Wonder Bread*, along with peanut butter, grape jelly, and the menu for our after-church lunch. An understandable view, perhaps, if not scripturally accurate. In ancient Israel the only *Wonder Bread* was manna. Regular bread was homemade, sometimes unleavened, usually cooked in a pan or baked in a clay oven, and time-consuming to make.

Still, bread was such a staple of ancient Middle Eastern diets that words for bread—*LECHEM* in Hebrew and *ARTOS* in Greek—came to mean food in general, and by extension, daily provisions of all kinds. Even in our modern society, the term *bread-winner* is synonymous with family provider.

Martin Luther understood the words "daily bread" to mean "everything that belongs to the support and wants of the body, such as food, drink, clothing, shoes, house, home, field, cattle, money, goods, a pious spouse, pious children, pious servants, pious and faithful rulers, good government, good weather, peace, health, discipline, honor, good friends, faithful neighbors, and the like." Quite a list.

By "daily bread," then, Jesus meant *everything* we need to live on a daily basis. And where do all these blessings come from? God.

## Dependence on God

The psalmist wrote, "The eyes of all look expectantly to You, and You give them their food in due season. You open Your hand and satisfy the desire of every living thing," Psalm 145:15-16. The picture drawn by these verses is one of complete dependence on God.

Only, in our modern world of computers, cell phones, ATMs and government-funded programs, we don't always see, feel, or admit that dependence. We think, "I go to work; God doesn't. I buy the groceries and pay the bills; God doesn't. The corporate comptroller signs my paychecks; God doesn't. The paychecks read BANK OF AMERICA, not BANK OF HEAVEN."

Yet, who makes the sun shine and the rain fall so that crops grow, livestock is fed, and you and I have food on our tables? Who gives us ears to hear, eyes to see, minds to think, air to breathe, food to eat, water to drink, families to love, jobs to hold? The list is endless, as endless as God's love and benevolence. If we made time to ponder the items on this list, even one item per day, we would realize how dependent we are on God for everything, including daily bread—and yes, even *Wonder Bread*.

## Trust in God

However, the words "give us this day our daily bread" not only show our dependence on God, they also invite us to trust in God. We may wonder, "Why didn't Jesus tell us to pray for a monthly supply of bread, or a biannual supply of bread, or even a lifetime supply of bread, groceries, bottled water, clothes, shoes, gasoline, laundry detergent, or whatever else we may need?"

Instead, Jesus taught us to ask for *daily* bread. In fact, He emphasized the daily allotment twice, saying both "this day" and "daily bread." Though not readily apparent in English, the Greek construction of this verse is even more emphatic: literally, "give us what is sufficient for today every day." Furthermore, the verb *give* in this verse is in the present tense, a tense of continuous action. In other words, "Lord, *always* provide for us in this way. Give us what we need each day, every day."

Here there is an unmistakable reference to the forty years the Israelites wandered in the wilderness—a sun-scorched land of snakes, scorpions and spiders, but no food or water. Throughout those forty years, God fed His people with "daily bread" from heaven. Not knowing what to call the bread, the Israelites named it *manna*, meaning, "What is it?"

Everything about manna defined it as a daily provision from God. Manna appeared from heaven once each day. Once each day, the Israelites gathered as much manna as they needed—with the exception of Friday, when they collected twice the amount in preparation for the Sabbath Day. Manna was so much of a daily provision, that any manna kept for more than one day, other than that gathered on Friday, instantly grew maggoty and smelly.

Why did God feed His people on a *per diem* basis? The answer is provided in Deuteronomy 8:3, where Moses reminded the Israelites, God "humbled you, allowed you to hunger, and fed you with manna which you did not know nor did your fathers know, that He might make you know that man shall not live by bread alone; but man lives by every word that proceeds from the mouth of the LORD."

In that dry, inhospitable wilderness, where the Israelites were unable to plant, cultivate, or harvest, God fed them daily and miraculously. One look outside the tent flap, and the Israelites knew with no doubt Who led them, Who fed them, Who loved them: God. Jesus taught this same important lesson with His "give us this day our daily bread" of the Lord's

Prayer. And the lesson is that we are utterly dependent on God, and we can utterly trust God.

And why can we utterly trust God? Because He is utterly reliable? Yes. Because He is eternally faithful? Yes. But also because, as Jesus taught in the introduction of the Lord's Prayer, God is our heavenly Father. And it is this Father who invites us to pray, "Give us this day our daily bread."

Remember, this is the very same Father of whom Paul wrote in Romans 8:31-32, "If God is for us, who can be against us? He who did not spare His own Son, but delivered *Him* up for us all, how shall He not with Him also freely give us all things?"

Said another way, if our heavenly Father willingly sacrificed His only Son to redeem us, will He withhold any godly blessing from our lives? If He gave us Jesus, the Bread of Life, will He fail to provide us with daily bread?

THE FIFTH PETITION

# And Forgive Us Our Trespasses

Luke 11:4

*Because God daily and richly forgives us, we should also—what? The answer is obvious, isn't it?*

As Christians, everything we are, have, and anticipate is based solely on God's forgiveness in Jesus Christ. *Everything.*

Forgiveness is the reason Jesus came into the world. As Paul wrote in Ephesians 1:7, "In Him we have redemption through His blood, the forgiveness of sins, according to the riches of His grace."

Forgiveness is what God offers through the Means of Grace. Forgiveness through the Gospel. Forgiveness through Baptism. Forgiveness through the Lord's Supper, as Jesus said in Matthew 26:28, "For this is My blood of the new covenant, which is shed for many for the remission of sins."

The authority of the Christian Church to forgive and retain sins is an authority from Christ Himself. "Receive the Holy Spirit," said Jesus. "If you forgive the sins of any, they are forgiven them; if you retain the sins of any, they are retained," John 20:23.

Therefore, because God richly and daily forgives us, we should also—what? The answer is obvious, isn't it? Because God daily and richly forgives us, we should also forgive others. Indeed, in Scripture, these two principles, forgiven and forgiving, are inextricably linked.

Jesus taught this connection in the Lord's Prayer, saying, "And forgive us our sins, for we also forgive everyone who is indebted to us," Luke 11:4. And Paul made the same connection in Ephesians 4:32, "And be kind to one another, tenderhearted, forgiving one another, even as God in Christ forgave you."

But does this mean forgiving is easy? No. C.S. Lewis wrote: "Forgiveness is a wonderful word, until we have something to forgive."

## Obstacles to Forgiveness

Many obstacles stand in the way of forgiveness. For example, the *size* of an injury can impact our willingness to forgive. There are times in life when we are so hurt and so wronged, when so much is lost or taken away, we may feel it impossible to forgive.

The *consequences* of an injury can also impact our willingness to forgive. In 1978, I was injured in a city league basketball game in northern Minnesota. The result was extensive knee surgery and three months in a cast. Even though forty years have passed, I still feel the consequences of that injury on cold, damp winter days or when making a wrong step. Emotional injuries work in precisely the same way.

Likewise, the *frequency* of an injury can impact our willingness to forgive. Peter asked Jesus in Matthew 18: "Lord, how often shall my brother sin against me, and I forgive him? Up to seven times?" Most of us would consider forgiving the same person seven times for the same transgression an act of extreme generosity. But Jesus replied, "I do not say to you up to seven times, but up to seventy times seven."

And without question, our sinful nature is an obstacle to forgiveness. As Christians, we are no longer controlled by the Old Nature; rather, we are led by the Spirit of God. Still, our Old Nature remains with us, warring against all that is good and godly, including the desire to forgive.

Yet, despite the obstacles to forgiveness, no where does God say, "Forgive if you like," or "Forgive if you're in the mood," or "Forgive if you think it worth the effort." He simply says, "Forgive, as I have forgiven you." Or in the words of the Lord's Prayer: "Forgive us our trespasses, as we forgive those who trespass against us."

## The Strength to Forgive

It is a sinful world. And where sin exists, there also exists the certainty of injuring and being injured. Deliberately or accidentally, we all hurt others; and we are all hurt by others. And some of these injuries are beyond our personal strength to forgive. It may be the pain of a troubled marriage, the good reputation tarnished by gossip, the retirement pension lost by unscrupulous investors, or the life taken by a drunk driver.

The time will come when each of us struggles to forgive, when each of us recognizes that forgiveness is beyond our personal power. But it is not beyond God's power. And the Bible assures us that God never asks anything of us that He does not empower us to do, and that includes the power to forgive.

The strength to forgive does not come from within or from gauging the size, consequences, or frequency of an injury. No, the strength to forgive comes from our connection to Jesus Christ and the blood He shed for our forgiveness.

## The Willingness to Forgive

Jesus once told a parable about an unmerciful servant. This servant owed his master a vast sum of money. But having nothing with which to repay, he begged his master for mercy. And his master forgave the debt.

But that same servant found a fellow-servant who owed him a small amount of money. When this fellow-servant asked for leniency and time to repay the debt, the unmerciful servant refused and had him thrown into a debtor's prison.

Learning of this injustice, the master called for the unmerciful servant and said, "You wicked servant! I forgave you all that debt because you begged me. Should you not also have had compassion on your fellow servant, just as I had pity on you?" Matthew 18:32-33. Though forgiven, the unmerciful servant was unforgiving.

How much has God forgiven each of us? What did it cost Him to redeem us? When we answer these questions in light of Scripture—at the cross of Jesus Christ—surely, we will be willing to forgive others.

## The Standard of Forgiveness

*God's forgiveness is complete.* He never dredges up the past. He keeps no record of wrongs. "If You, LORD, should mark iniquities, O Lord, who could stand? But there is forgiveness with You, that You may be feared," Psalm 130:3-4.

*God's forgiveness is unconditional;* that is, it is not conditioned by anything we must do to merit His forgiveness. What can we do? What payment can we make to atone for the massive debt of our sins? Absolutely nothing. Rather, God forgives us freely for Christ's sake, out of undeserved love and grace—as stated in Isaiah 43:25, "I, even I, am He who blots out your transgressions for My own sake; and I will not remember your sins."

*God's forgiveness is limitless.* He always forgives us when we turn to Him in repentance and faith. The psalmist wrote, "He has not dealt with us according to our sins, nor punished us according to our iniquities. For as the heavens are high above the earth, so great is His mercy toward those who fear Him; as far as the east is from the west, so far has He removed our transgressions from us," Psalm 103:10-12.

Martin Luther's explanation of the Fifth Petition in the Lord's Prayer is simple and beautiful. He said, "We pray in this petition that our Father in heaven would not look upon our sins, nor on their account deny our prayer; for we are worthy of none of the things for which we pray, neither have we deserved them; but that He would grant them all to us by grace; for we daily sin much and indeed deserve nothing but punishment. So will we also heartily forgive, and readily do good to others."

# And Lead Us Not into Temptation

## Luke 11:4

*God is a holy God and tempts no one. But why then did Jesus teach us to pray, "And lead us not into temptation"?*

"And lead us not into temptation." Has this petition ever puzzled you, perhaps even troubled you—the thought that God would actually lead us into temptation?

God is a holy God, sinless and perfect, intolerant of sin. He told the Israelites, "You shall be holy, for I the LORD your God am holy," Leviticus 19:2. Or as stated in Proverbs 15:9, "The way of the wicked is an abomination to the LORD, but He loves him who follows righteousness."

Clearly, God cannot abide sin. God cannot be tempted by sin. And God tempts no one with sin. As James wrote, "Let no one say when he is tempted, 'I am tempted by God'; for God cannot be tempted by evil, nor does He Himself tempt anyone. But each one is tempted when he is drawn away by his own desires and enticed," James 1:13-14.

Furthermore, God is not only the holy God, He is also our loving Father through Jesus Christ. Jesus emphasized this relationship when teaching us to pray. "When you pray, say: Our Father in heaven," Luke 11:2. By the time we recite the Sixth Petition, "And lead us not into temptation," we've already confessed that God is our Father, that His name is sacred, that His kingdom brings salvation, that He provides for all our needs, and that He forgives all our sins.

But precisely here we reach that head-scratching question: Would such a heavenly Father ever lead His children into temptation? Would He, figuratively speaking, bait a hook with evil and wait for us to bite? Would He set traps, bury landmines, drop banana peels? Of course not.

Why then did Jesus teach us to pray, "And lead us not into temptation"? Have we misunderstood His words? No. The age-old translation is the correct one. In the two places where the Sixth Petition is recorded in Scripture, Matthew 6:13 and Luke 11:4, the same Greek words are used—identical words, identical word order, identical meaning.

So, what is the meaning of "And lead us not into temptation"?

### God is not the Source of Temptation

Consider the words of the Sixth Petition carefully: "And lead us not into temptation." Do these words teach or even suggest that God is the one tempting us, or that God is the originator or owner of the temptation? Not in the least. The temptation already exists.

In reality, temptation is always near: at home, work, and school; on TV, radio, and the internet; in movies and books; on flashing neon signs and large freeway billboards; when walking the dog or even singing in church.

In the 1960s, TV censorship was considerable. For example, in every bedroom scene of the old, black-and-white sitcom, *The Dick Van Dyke Show*, actors playing the parts of husband and wife were required to wear full-length pajamas, and if lying in the same bed to keep at least one foot on the floor. Fast-forward to 2018. Today's programming offers a smorgasbord of murder, mayhem, nudity, homosexuality, same-sex marriage, four-letter rants, God-mocking, and Christian-bashing—all before 9:00 P.M.

In fact, temptation is so pervasive that it gladly comes to us. No "leading" is necessary. It slithers in like a serpent. It leaps in like a roaring lion as Peter warned in his first epistle: "Be sober, be vigilant; because your adversary the devil walks about like a roaring lion, seeking whom he may devour,"

1 Peter 5:8.

If it were God's intention to lead us into temptation, how much leading would He have to do? Little to none. At times, we even lead ourselves—wide-eyed, straining forward at full-throttle. Temptation is everywhere. And we need no one to lead us into it, least of all God. This is not a theological argument, but it is a compelling one.

## God is the Leader

While it's easy to dwell on the "lead us not" part of the Sixth Petition, our real focus should be on the *Leader*, not the leading. For when we truly know Who is leading us—the holy God Who hates sin, the loving Father Who atoned for sin by sacrificing His only Son—we'll also know that He would never lead us into temptation. His design is to lead us away from temptation, to protect us from it, and to deliver us should we fall into it. Hence we pray, "And lead us not into temptation, *but* deliver us from evil."

Many Greek grammarians refer to the verb "lead" in "lead us not into temptation" as a permissive imperative. *Permissive* has to do with permission. This verb then has more to do with *letting* than with *leading*.

In other words, when we pray, "And lead us not into temptation," we're asking our heavenly Father to prevent us from falling into temptation by giving us the wisdom and strength to resist it; and by keeping us from going places we shouldn't go, saying things we shouldn't say, watching things we shouldn't watch, or doing anything that would allow the devil, world, or our own sinful nature to exploit our weaknesses.

The meaning of the Sixth Petition, then, is remarkably similar to that which Jesus told His disciples in the Garden of Gethsemane: "Pray that you may not enter into temptation," Luke 22:40.

## God is Faithful

When we pray, "And lead us not into temptation," we are merely asking God to do what He has already promised to do. The same is true of all the other petitions of the Lord's Prayer. There are many places in Scripture where God has promised to hallow His name, extend His kingdom, carry out His will, provide for all our needs, forgive all our sins, and protect and deliver us from evil.

Thus, the Sixth Petition should not puzzle or trouble us, but rather hearten us. For in it we're simply reminding God, and in so doing reminding ourselves, of something He has promised He would never do; namely, lead us into temptation. Tempting is Satan's business. Salvation is God's.

In the words of Paul: "God is faithful, who will not allow you to be tempted beyond what you are able, but with the temptation will also make the way of escape, that you may be able to bear it," 1 Corinthians 10:13. And in 2 Timothy 4:18, "And the Lord will deliver me from every evil work and preserve me for His heavenly kingdom. To Him be the glory forever and ever. Amen."

Or in the words of Martin Luther: "God indeed tempts no one; but we pray in this petition that God would guard and keep us, so that the devil, the world, and our flesh may not deceive us nor seduce us into misbelief, despair, and other great shame and vice; and though we be assailed by them, that still we may finally overcome and obtain the victory."

# But Deliver Us from Evil

## Luke 11:4

*The words of this petition may be familiar and few, but they have much to teach about the nature of evil and the source of our deliverance.*

"But deliver us from evil." This seventh and final petition is a fitting epilogue to all the other petitions. Martin Luther referred to it as a summary, writing, "We pray in this petition, *as the sum of all,* that our Father in heaven would deliver us from every evil of body and soul, property and honor, and finally, when our last hour has come, grant us a blessed end, and graciously take us from this vale of tears to Himself in heaven."

Though the words of this petition are familiar and few, they nevertheless have much to teach about the nature of evil and the source of our deliverance.

### Deliver Us from Evil

In the Seventh Petition, the Greek word for evil, *PONAROS,* means both moral evil and physical evil; wicked behavior and bad news. Obviously, the two are related. At the Fall of Adam and Eve, moral evil or disobedience to God brought sin; sin brought pain, hardship, loss, futility, and death. In fact, that Greek word for evil, *PONAROS,* comes from another Greek word meaning pain.

The evil in our world is evident and everywhere, in the daily papers and on the nightly news: murders, ethnic cleansings, cruel dictators, serial killers, drug peddlers, child pornographers, Hitlers and holocausts; terrorists who bomb, butcher, behead, and burn, then place their bloody handiwork on the internet in high definition. This is pure evil; and the evil causes enormous pain.

The natural disasters labeled as "Acts of God"—the plagues, earthquakes, floods, mudslides, tornados, blizzards, and droughts—are not truly God's acts, though He may allow them. This is not the world God created for us, but a world we doomed and darkened through sin. Pointedly, God told Adam, "Cursed is the ground *for your sake,*" Genesis 3:17.

In the Seventh Petition we ask God to deliver us from all forms of evil—whether evil people or evil events—that may injure our bodies or injure our faith, and in so doing, drive us to doubt and despair. As Luther said, "every evil of body and soul, property and honor."

This is why we pray, "But deliver us from evil."

## Deliver Us from the Evil One

Evil has an origin, and the ultimate originator of evil is the devil. Though we commonly recite the Seventh Petition as "but deliver us from evil," in the two passages where this petition is recorded—Matthew 6:13 and Luke 11:4—the Greek is more literally "but deliver us from the *evil one,*" that is, the devil.

Many deny the existence of the devil. Some view him as a myth; others, merely a symbol of evil; and still others, a laughable caricature with two horns, burnt-red skin, arrowed tail, cloven hooves, sharp pitchfork, and fine Cuban cigar. Funny. Comical. HA-HA-HA. Frankly, the devil is the one laughing at those who find him cuddly, pudgy, harmless, and nonexistent.

At the other extreme are people who not only believe in the devil but worship him as their god. A god of no rules. A god of no expectations other than eat, drink, be merry and sin, sex, and self. In 1966, the nation was stunned when Anton Lavey founded the Church of Satan in San Francisco, California. Oh, how times have changed. In 2016, a member of the Temple of Satan opened a city council meeting in Pensacola, Florida with a satanic invocation.

The devil is real. He isn't cartoonish, pudgy, horned, hooved, or pitchforked. He is a powerful, malignant spirit whose only focus is to destroy faith in Jesus and swallow souls. Peter wrote in his First Epistle, "Be sober, be vigilant; because your adversary the devil walks about like a roaring lion, seeking whom he may devour. Resist him, steadfast in the faith," 1 Peter 5:8-9.

Thank God, the devil is now a defeated enemy through the atoning death and resurrection of our Savior, Jesus Christ. Satan "can harm us none," Luther wrote in his great Reformation hymn. "He's judged; the deed is done. One little word can fell him." And that "little" word is the all-powerful Word of God.

However, though a defeated enemy, the devil is still *our* enemy. Whether he strikes like a serpent or hunts like a ravenous lion, he is too strong and too clever for us to oppose him on our own. This is why Paul told the Ephesians, "Put on the whole armor of God, that you may be able to stand against the wiles of the devil. For we do not wrestle against flesh and blood, but against principalities, against powers, against the rulers of the darkness of this age, against spiritual hosts of wickedness in the heavenly places," Ephesians 6:11-12.

On our own, we can't defeat the devil. When we are in Christ by faith, the devil can't defeat us. God has promised to deliver us. And this is why we pray, "But deliver us from the evil one."

### Deliver Us from Ourselves

Though we are children of God and led by His Spirit, in this life we still have the Old Sinful Nature, and that nature wars against all that is good and godly. Paul himself described the War Within, saying in Romans 7, "For what I am doing, I do not understand. For what I will to do, that I do not practice; but what I hate, that I do. . . . But I see another law in my members, *warring* against the law of my mind."

The world, the devil, and our own sinful nature make a

powerful Triumvirate, which we cannot defeat on our own. This, too, is why we pray, "But deliver us from evil."

## Deliver Us, O God

When we pray "but deliver us from evil," we are not only asking God to deliver us, we are simultaneously admitting that we cannot deliver ourselves. This may be an obvious lesson, but it is also a very important lesson—especially in view of the difficulties, evil, and evil one that we face in life.

Nowhere does Scripture tell us to confront evil, loss, or hardship on our own. Instead, it begins with a warning, "Therefore let him who thinks he stands take heed lest he fall"; and it ends with a glorious promise: "God is faithful, who will not allow you to be tempted beyond what you are able, but with the temptation will also make the way of escape, that you may be able to bear it," 1 Corinthians 10:12-13.

When attacked by Gospel-haters and assailed by Satan, Paul did not say, "I can handle this." He said, "I can do all things through Christ who strengthens me," Philippians 4:13. He didn't say, "I will deliver myself"; rather, "And the Lord will deliver me from every evil work and preserve me for His heavenly kingdom," 2 Timothy 4:18.

Our heavenly Father is our heavenly Deliverer. Of His own love and volition, and in answer to our prayers, He will deliver us from evil and the evil one. He will deliver us from every evil that would dishonor His name, hinder His kingdom, oppose His gracious will, and move us to despair, until that glorious hour when He grants us a blessed end and graciously takes us "from this vale of tears to Himself in heaven."

This is why we pray, "But deliver us from evil." This is why we bow our heads and say with grateful hearts, "For Thine is the kingdom and the power and the glory forever and ever. Amen."

THE CONCLUSION

# For Thine Is the Kingdom and the Power and the Glory

Matthew 6:13

*The word "for" in the conclusion of the Lord's Prayer explains why we pray with such certainty: the kingdom is God's, the power is God's, the glory is God's.*

The introduction of the Lord's Prayer teaches us how to pray; namely, in view of a wondrous relationship: "Our Father who art in heaven." Through the atoning sacrifice of Christ, God the Father is now *our* Father; our *ABBA*, a term of endearment and trust. And as our Father, He wants us to approach Him freely and with great confidence, knowing that He Himself has invited us to pray and has promised to answer.

The seven petitions of the Lord's Prayer teach us what to pray; that is, important things to pray for: the hallowing of God's name, the coming of God's Kingdom, the doing of God's will, our daily bread, forgiveness, protection from temptation, and deliverance from evil. But along with these petitions, our heavenly Father wants us to bring petitions of our own. He wants to hear everything—our joys and sorrows, our successes and failures, our wants and worries, how school went, how the car is running, how our marriage is doing.

And so Paul told the Philippians, "Be anxious for nothing, but in everything by prayer and supplication, with thanksgiving, let your requests be made known to God; and the peace of God, which surpasses all understanding, will guard your hearts and minds through Christ Jesus," Philippians 4:6-7.

In the conclusion of the Lord's Prayer we pray, "For Thine

is the kingdom and the power and the glory forever and ever. Amen." Notice that little word "for". It explains why we can pray to God with such certainty. The kingdom is God's. The power is God's. The glory is God's.

## Thine Is the Kingdom

In the Second Petition we pray, "Thy kingdom come." *This* kingdom refers specifically to God's gracious rule in human hearts through the power of the Gospel—an internal kingdom, invisible to us but known to God. A kingdom not made of borders and buildings but of believing hearts.

However, the "kingdom" mentioned in the conclusion of the Lord's Prayer is far more than God's rule in human hearts. It embraces God's sovereign rule over the entire universe and everything in it, from the smallest subatomic particle to the largest constellation; every nation, every ruler, every breath, every heartbeat, every relationship, every illness, and every problem.

The meaning of "Thine is the kingdom" is beautifully expressed in 1 Chronicles 29:10-12, where David writes, "Blessed are You, LORD God of Israel, our Father, forever and ever. Yours, O LORD, is the greatness, the power and the glory, the victory and the majesty; for all that is in heaven and in earth is Yours; Yours is the kingdom, O LORD, and You are exalted as head over all. Both riches and honor come from You, and You reign over all. In Your hand is power and might; in Your hand it is to make and to give strength to all."

Our God reigns supreme over everything, including those worries and burdens we present to Him in prayer. The kingdom is God's. The comfort is ours.

## Thine Is the Power

"I believe in God the Father Almighty, Maker of heaven and earth." The words are from the Apostles' Creed; a creed many of us use on Sundays to confess our faith. "God is almighty," we say. "God has all power." And no sooner do we leave the church building, start the car, turn right or left at the next intersection, and speed off toward our personal problems and burdens—serious illness, troubled marriage, financial difficulties—we're already acting as if we had never spoken the words; or worse, as if God had no power at all.

"Thine is the kingdom *and the power*," we pray, and for good reason. The words remind us that no problem, no burden, or no petition is too hard for the Lord.

When God promised Abraham and Sarah a son, Abraham's body was reproductively dead and Sarah was elderly, barren, and beyond the age of childbearing. In that setting of human impossibility, God asked Abraham and Sarah this question: "Is anything too hard for the LORD?" Well, is it? Of course not.

When you think your problems are too big for God to solve, remember these words of Jesus: "with God all things are possible." Remember the words of the hymnist: "Thou art coming to a King, large petitions with thee bring; for His grace and power are such, none can ever ask too much."

The power is God's. The comfort is ours.

## Thine Is the Glory

Surely, this phrase needs no explanation. It flows inevitably from everything that has gone before it: that God is our Father through the sacrifice of His only Son; that through the preaching of His name, His word, we are now a part of His kingdom; that day after day He provides for all our needs; that He forgives all our sins, leads us away from temptation, delivers us from evil; that He controls all things and works all things to serve our best interests; and that He does all this out of undeserved love and grace, apart from any worth or works of our own.

The question is not, "Should we give glory to God?" Rather, the question is, "How can we fail or forget to glorify God?" As David wrote, "Give unto the LORD the glory due His name; worship the LORD in the beauty of holiness," Psalm

29:2.

The glory is God's. The blessings are ours.

## Amen

"Amen" is the last word of the Lord's Prayer. "Amen" is also the last word in twenty-four of the twenty-seven New Testament Books. The Israelites were required to say "amen" at the end of each curse read from Mount Ebal. Paul closed his doxology in Romans 11:36 with "amen." Peter did the same in 1 Peter 5:11.

We're so used to seeing, saying, singing, or hearing "amen" at the end of things—creeds, hymns, prayers, sermons—we may conclude that "amen" means THE END. This is where we stop singing. This is where the preacher stops preaching.

Only, look carefully, and you'll find Jesus saying "amen" at the beginning of important statements too, and sometimes using the word twice for emphasis. Though usually translated as "truly, truly" or "verily, verily" or "most assuredly," the actual word used is "amen."

"Amen" is from the Hebrew verb *AMAN*, which means to prop up, support, stay, and sustain. "Amen" then expresses absolute certainty and conviction. It's a solemn affirmation of truth, and therefore the reason Jesus used it to close the Lord's Prayer.

In Luther's words: "I should be certain that these petitions are acceptable to our Father in heaven, and are heard by Him; for He Himself has commanded us to pray, and has promised to hear us. Amen, Amen, that is, Yea, yea, it shall be so."

## OTHER BOOKS BY
## MARK WEIS

### Available on Amazon.com

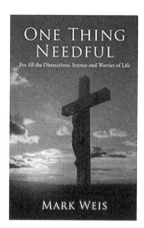

ONE THING NEEDFUL
Volume 1

We have many needs in life. Yet, according to Jesus, only one thing is most needful; namely, staying close to His Word. Through His Word, God blesses, saves, provides hope and spiritual healing. Can you think of anything more important or more needful?

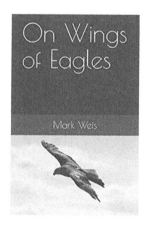

ON WINGS OF EAGLES

*On Wings of Eagles* is a collection of Christian devotions and poetry written by the author over twenty-seven years. Devotions and poems are based on Scripture passages and flavored with the author's personal experiences. Easy to read, this book applies the truths of Scripture to the realities of daily life, with the intent of providing hope, joy, and encouragement.

Made in the USA
Middletown, DE
09 October 2018